Johannes Brahms

A Biographical Sketch

HERMANN DEITERS

CAMBRIDGE UNIVERSITY PRESS

Cambridge, New York, Melbourne, Madrid, Cape Town, Singapore,
São Paolo, Delhi, Dubai, Tokyo

Published in the United States of America by Cambridge University Press, New York

www.cambridge.org
Information on this title: www.cambridge.org/9781108004794

© in this compilation Cambridge University Press 2009

This edition first published 1888
This digitally printed version 2009

ISBN 978-1-108-00479-4 Paperback

This book reproduces the text of the original edition. The content and language reflect
the beliefs, practices and terminology of their time, and have not been updated.

Cambridge University Press wishes to make clear that the book, unless originally published
by Cambridge, is not being republished by, in association or collaboration with, or
with the endorsement or approval of, the original publisher or its successors in title.

CAMBRIDGE LIBRARY COLLECTION
Books of enduring scholarly value

Music

The systematic academic study of music gave rise to works of description, analysis and criticism, by composers and performers, philosophers and anthropologists, historians and teachers, and by a new kind of scholar - the musicologist. This series makes available a range of significant works encompassing all aspects of the developing discipline.

Johannes Brahms

Hermann Deiters (1833–1907) first met Brahms in 1856, and became an enthusiastic supporter of his work. This 'biographical sketch' was published in English in 1888, edited by J.A. Fuller Maitland, the English musicologist whose Robert Schumann in the Novello 'Great Musicians' series and Masters of German Music are also reissued in this series. Brahms was still alive and composing at this time: the book consists of a short account of his life followed by a critical review of all his works up to 1887. The preface states: 'That Johannes Brahms is by far the greatest composer of our time ... will not be contested by any musician whose claim to an opinion is based on an exhaustive knowledge of his works. ... Brahms has a place in the line of supreme masters in the craft of music, that line which stretches down without interruption through Palestrina, from a far earlier time.'

Cambridge University Press has long been a pioneer in the reissuing of out-of-print titles from its own backlist, producing digital reprints of books that are still sought after by scholars and students but could not be reprinted economically using traditional technology. The Cambridge Library Collection extends this activity to a wider range of books which are still of importance to researchers and professionals, either for the source material they contain, or as landmarks in the history of their academic discipline.

Drawing from the world-renowned collections in the Cambridge University Library, and guided by the advice of experts in each subject area, Cambridge University Press is using state-of-the-art scanning machines in its own Printing House to capture the content of each book selected for inclusion. The files are processed to give a consistently clear, crisp image, and the books finished to the high quality standard for which the Press is recognised around the world. The latest print-on-demand technology ensures that the books will remain available indefinitely, and that orders for single or multiple copies can quickly be supplied.

The Cambridge Library Collection will bring back to life books of enduring scholarly value (including out-of-copyright works originally issued by other publishers) across a wide range of disciplines in the humanities and social sciences and in science and technology.

JOHANNES BRAHMS.

Johannes Brahms.

JOHANNES BRAHMS

A Biographical Sketch.

BY

DR. HERMANN DEITERS

TRANSLATED, WITH ADDITIONS
BY
ROSA NEWMARCH

EDITED WITH A PREFACE
BY J. A. FULLER MAITLAND

London
T. FISHER UNWIN
26 PATERNOSTER SQUARE
MDCCCLXXXVIII

EDITOR'S PREFACE.

CONTEMPORARY biography has its obvious disadvantages, more especially when its subject is still living, and in the possession of fullest vigour of work ; but it has its own advantages to compensate for these. That it should take the form of personal reminiscences is greatly to be desired, since the peculiar merit of a contemporary account is more likely to be brought out by this than by any other method. Dr. Deiters has adopted this style in the short account which he prefixes to his critical review of all the works of Brahms, and there is no doubt that when the time comes for writing the composer's life—long may it be before the materials for such a work are completed by the master's death!— his biographer will find one of his most valuable sources of information in the book which is here presented in an English dress. The biographical part of the work is of necessity short, for not one of the giants of music has had so uneventful a career as has fallen to the lot of Brahms, if we except Sebastian Bach, with whom, in this and many other respects, our master may be fitly compared. Since there is no prospect of our seeing the greatest composer of our time in England, we might well have expected a little more information as to his actual outward appearance and manner; but we must thankfully accept what we can get, and not grumble because the author has chosen to emphasize the important features of his compositions rather than to dwell upon the colour of his hair or the cut of his clothes.

That Johannes Brahms is by far the greatest composer of our time—taking that term in a wide sense, as including all the period since the death of Schumann

—will not be contested by any musician whose claim to an opinion is based on an exhaustive knowledge of his works. Musical fanatics of various schools have attempted to institute comparisons between Brahms and Wagner, ignoring the fact that there is no possible standard by which their relative magnitudes can be measured. In the art, or rather in the combination of arts, which he himself invented, Wagner stands without a rival, and it is scarcely possible that a legitimate successor to his vacant throne will ever arise; but he could no more have written the *Deutsches Requiem*, or the four symphonies, than Brahms could have created *Parsifal*. Brahms has a place in the line of supreme masters in the craft of music, that line which stretches down without interruption through Palestrina, from a far earlier time. To compare him with his predecessors in that illustrious category would be, as Dr. Deiters says, an idle task; suffice it to say that the prophetic mantle handed on to him by Robert Schumann, has in him found no unworthy wearer.

The manner in which the book has been rendered into English needs no apology, but it may be premised that the translator has chosen rather to reproduce as faithfully as possible the style of the original, than to clothe the author's thoughts in words which might perhaps fall less strangely upon English ears. The additional matter, in which the compositions of Brahms' later years are reviewed, will, it is hoped, be especially welcome to those whose admiration for the master's work is of recent growth, and who have had few opportunities of becoming acquainted with his earlier compositions. The complete catalogue appended to the translation does not appear in the original.

JOHANNES BRAHMS.

It was in the middle of the fifties—if we are not mistaken, in the summer of 1856—that we first met in Bonn a young musician whose whole demeanour at once distinguished him from the rest of his youthful companions. Not that he was remarkable for that external freedom of manner common among artists, which, however, seldom arouses our sympathy. He seemed, on the contrary, unconcerned by the world around him, filled with an artistic ideal, absorbed in striving after some conscious aim, yet ready to share freely and amiably with others the treasures of his artistic convictions. A common interest had guided us both to the spot where the great master, so heartily honoured by all the young school—Robert Schumann—was then living, overshadowed by his heavy affliction. The young artist was eager to see the master whom he, too, so highly revered. If his natural enthusiastic manner pleased at first sight, much more did one learn to like him on hearing him speak with sincere veneration of the great master's ideas, and of their relations towards each other. This young artist was *Johannes Brahms*. Although at that time he was little known to the general public, those who were truly interested in the history of music had shortly before had their attention drawn to him by the glowing prophetic words with which Schumann himself had introduced him into the ranks of creative artists. These words, gladly acquiesced in by some, called forth criticism and contradiction from others — even from earnest men of artistic culture—who could not at once reconcile themselves to the peculiar style of Brahms' earliest compositions.

As in all such cases, a considerable time must elapse before the public could be convinced that it had now to deal with an original, important, and entirely novel figure. From that time forward, however, we find Brahms, himself unmoved by these diverse criticisms, pursuing with sure and steady steps the aim he had so clearly in view.

The outward life of the artist has been a somewhat uneventful one.

Johannes Brahms was born at Hamburg on May 7, 1833. His father, a contrabassist in the orchestra of the town theatre, was also an able performer on several other instruments. Growing up in a musical family and among musical surroundings, Brahms early displayed his remarkable talent as a pianist; and thus we see in his case a repetition of an occurrence so often observed in the history of music. His first master, for the piano, was D. Cossel of Hamburg. He also began early with theoretical studies, and even in his boyhood felt the necessity of penetrating the organic structure of musical works. We recollect his telling us that before he really knew how to score thoroughly, he used to practise putting long pieces from single parts into full score. He carried on his theoretical studies systematically under Ed. Marxsen of Altona (also celebrated through Schumann), to whose direction was due his great improvement as a pianist. Assisted by his already mature and astonishing memory, he made rapid progress, and early in life entered deeply into the spirit of the classical masters, among whom he decidedly adopted Bach and Beethoven as his models. At the age of fourteen he played for the first time in public, and met with great applause. The programme included his own "Variations on a Volkslied," and its appearance at that important moment of his career shows us clearly that a predilection for the national element in music was, even in those early days, deeply rooted in his heart.

In 1853 he left home to accompany the Hungarian violinist Remenyi on a concert tour. During his tour he visited, among other places, Hanover, Göttingen, and Weimar; and by his playing and compositions attracted the attention of Joachim and Liszt. The former was especially struck when, in Göttingen, on account of the low pitch of the piano, Brahms transposed Beethoven's Kreutzer Sonata, without having the notes before him, from A into B flat. This success resulted in his severing his connection with Remenyi, and going to Düsseldorf in October, 1853, with an introduction from Joachim to Robert Schumann. He had then composed several grand sonatas for piano, a scherzo for piano (which had especially gained Liszt's approbation), and a considerable number of songs. Schumann's enthusiasm at the first chords Brahms struck on the piano, an enthusiasm which increased with every fresh hearing, has been repeatedly described; he believed most confidently that he saw in this young man the ideal whose advent he had so long awaited. In an article in the "Neue Zeitschrift für Musik," entitled "New Paths," he announced this new apparition to the musical world. His words have been frequently quoted before, but we must repeat their substance once again. "Ten years have passed away," he writes—"almost as many as I formerly devoted to the publication of this paper—since I have allowed myself to commit my opinions to this soil, so rich in memories. Often, in spite of an overstrained productive activity, I have felt moved to do so; many new and remarkable talents made their appearance, and a fresh musical power seemed about to reveal itself among the many aspiring artists of the day, even if their compositions were only known to the few. I thought to follow with interest the pathways of these elect; there would—there must—after such promise, suddenly appear one who should utter the highest ideal expression of the times, who should claim the mastership by no gradual development, but burst upon us fully equipped, as Minerva sprang from the brain of Jupiter. And he has come, this chosen youth, over whose cradle the Graces and Heroes seem to have kept watch. His name is *Johannes Brahms;* he comes from Hamburg, where he has been working in quiet obscurity, instructed by an excellent, enthusiastic teacher in the most difficult principles of his art, and lately introduced to me by an honoured and well-known master. His mere outward appearance assures us that he is one of the elect. Seated at the piano, he disclosed wondrous regions. We were drawn into an enchanted circle. Then came a moment of inspiration which transformed the piano into an orchestra of wailing and jubilant voices. There were sonatas, or rather veiled symphonies, songs whose poetry revealed itself without the aid of words, while throughout them all ran a vein of deep song-melody, several pieces of a half-demoniacal character, but of charming form, then sonatas for piano and violin, string-quartets, and each one of these creations so different from the last, that they appeared to flow from so many separate sources. Then, like an impetuous torrent, he seemed to unite these streams into a foaming waterfall; over the tossing waves the rainbow presently stretches its peaceful arch, while on the banks butterflies flit to and fro, and the nightingale warbles her song. Whenever he bends his magic wand towards great works, and the powers of orchestra and chorus lend him their aid, still more wonderful glimpses of the ideal world will be revealed to us. May the Highest Genius help him onward! Meanwhile another genius — that of modesty — seems to dwell within him. His comrades greet him at his first step in the world, where wounds may perhaps await him, but the bay and the laurel also; we welcome this valiant warrior."

The moment seems now to have come when we may judge the truth of these prophetic words, which at the time of their utterance no one but an artist of Schumann's own standing was in a position to do. It is easy to understand how they helped to determine the young artist's resolution and future development, so that he ever remained a devoted friend to the great master, and after his death kept an equally warm affection for his widow and family.

In the winter of the same year Brahms went to Leipzig and played there in public on December 17th. About this time the publishing firms of Breitkopf and Härtel and B. Senff resolved to bring out his first works: three grand sonatas for piano (op. 1, 2, and 5), a scherzo for piano (op. 4), several collections of songs and Lieder (op. 3, 6, 7), and a trio for piano, violin, and violoncello (op. 8), followed shortly by variations on a theme of

Schumann's (op. 9), and in 1856 by four ballades for piano (op. 10). In 1854, after spending a few weeks with Liszt at Weimar, passing some time in Hanover and other places, and undertaking several concert tours, he accepted the post of music-master and director of the choir to the Prince of Lippe-Detmold, which tied him for the winter months. He refused a situation which was offered him just then in the Rhenish conservatoire at Cologne. The former post gave him time and opportunity to strengthen and deepen his theoretical studies, and to increase his experience in the practical employment and management of great choral masses. This was undoubtedly the great transition period of his life; a time of earnest self-examination and severe study. If in his early works he may be reproached for a lavish expenditure of strength, a certain license of imagination, and a tendency to overstep the line of beauty by his daring combinations (though in the meantime Schumann accorded him unlimited praise), he shows his genuine artistic nature in the fact that neither severe criticism nor unbounded approval turned him from the straight road to the goal he had before him, nor hindered him from striving as he went to conquer all his besetting faults. The study of Brahms' earlier and later works will clearly show the successful result of these efforts.

After a few years he resigned the above-mentioned post, and for a time resided in his native town Hamburg, and afterwards in Switzerland, where, through Theodor Kirchner's introduction, he found a circle of warm admirers. For some years no new compositions made their appearance. In January, 1859, he played in Leipzig his concerto for piano (afterwards published as op. 15), but without success. In 1860 and 1861 he published the two Serenades for Orchestra, and several collections of songs for one or more voices, choruses, compositions for piano, and chamber-music, including the two sextets, of which the first appeared in 1862. A remarkable increase of artistic power and conviction is displayed in all these works. To attain beauty of form and clearness of expression is the fixed principle which henceforth governs his creations; and imagination must bow down before it and give way to a sober and dignified moderation. The productions of this period, beginning with op. 11 (Serenade, in D major), of almost Haydn-like straightforwardness and simplicity, offer a strange contrast to Brahms' earlier works. These, together with his studies in the strictest forms of Bach's school, which resulted in several small sacred compositions, were to many no less astonishing than the productions of his overflowing and youthful imagination.

To the attentive observer there can be no doubt that the original power and genius which shows itself in his early works is not extinguished, but, on the contrary, shines out more clearly though tempered by true, artistic moderation. In 1862 Brahms chose as a fixed home Vienna, that old capital of German music, made famous by so many great masters. Here he speedily gained many friends and followers, as much by his wonderful playing as by his compositions. At his recitals, besides his own works, he showed a preference for those of Bach, Beethoven, Schubert, and Schumann. There appeared, about this time, a series of important compositions, some of which may be described as studies in the severe school. In the year 1863 he became director of the Vienna Choral Society (Singakademie), in which position he was active in performing Bach's music; but he resigned the post in 1864. We now find him taking frequent journeys, and staying in those towns which were favourable to quiet hard work; among them he had a great predilection for Baden-Baden. As the result of this busy time appeared the two first quartets for Pf. (1863), the grand quintet for piano (1865), the trio for Pf., violin and horn; the sonata for piano and violoncello (1866), the variations on a theme of Paganini's, the waltzes for pianoforte duet, and a great many songs, among others, the Romances from Tieck's "Magelone." In the latter part of 1865 we meet him by the Rhine, when he conducted the first Serenade at Cologne; and in 1866, after a long concert tour in Switzerland, he returned to Vienna. Here, at the close of 1867, were performed the first three numbers of the *German Requiem*, conducted by Herbeck. The first full performance of this—so far his greatest—work was given (still without the 5th chorus) in Bremen Cathedral on April 10, 1868. It went the round of the principal German towns, exciting general admiration and appreciation. During a long stay in Bonn, in the summer of 1868, he busied himself with the publication of this work, put the finishing touches to the cantata *Rinaldo*, and again wrote a great number of songs, of which several collections (op. 43, op. 46–49) were published by Rieter-Biedermann of Leipzig, and Simrock of Berlin. It was at this time that the author of these lines enjoyed a constant and enthusiastic intercourse with the young artist, then at the full height of his power as a composer.

Shortly afterwards Brahms published the two string quartets (op. 51), the Liebeslieder Walzer (op. 52, 1869), and the Rhapsody after Goethe's Harzreise (op. 53). After spending the summer of 1869 in Baden-Baden, Vienna became once more the permanent scene of his labours, and since then his life has been quiet and uneventful, busied with the production of his works, and constantly devoted to composing: in the summer he retires to some quiet country resting-place.

In the winter of 1870–1871, inspired by the military feats of the German army, he composed the *Triumphlied*, to words from the Revelation of St. John. It was performed for the first time at Bremen, on Good Friday. Shortly afterwards the *Song of Fate* (Schicksalslied) was begun; in beauty and expression the most perfect of his smaller choral works. Since the winter of 1872 he had been directing the concerts of the "Gesellschaft der Musikfreunde." Meanwhile sympathy and admiration for the young composer was spreading in the musical world, and flattering acknowledgments of his talent were by no means wanting. We must mention the enthusiastic receptions accorded to him in the beginning of 1874, both at Leipzig and Munich, and also in May at Cologne, where the *Triumphlied* adorned the programme of the Lower Rhenish Musical Festival. This work was heard the same year in Breslau, and also in Berlin, through the influence of his friend Stockhausen. The King of Bavaria decorated him with the Maximilian Order of Arts and Science, the Academy of Arts of Berlin elected him a foreign member, together with Gade and Reinecke, and the Philosophical Faculty of the University of of Breslau awarded him the title of

Doctor of Philosophy, thus giving him precedence of all living composers of sacred music.

In 1875 he resigned the conductorship of the "Gesellschaft" concerts to Herbeck, and from that time has lived a life of unceasing productive activity, as the chief results of which we may point to the two great symphonies, the first of which in C minor (op. 68), was first performed at Carlsruhe on November 4, 1876; the second in D (op. 73), at Vienna, December 30, 1877. Besides these appeared a third piano quartet (op. 60, 1875), a third string-quartet (op. 67), a sonata for piano and violin (op. 78), and a violin concerto (op. 77), written for Joachim, and introduced by him to the musical world. In addition to the above-mentioned works were new collections of piano pieces and songs. Most of these new works were published by the old-established firm of Simrock, formerly of Bonn, but now of Berlin.

In 1880 Brahms conducted the performance given in memory of Robert Schumann at the unveiling of his monument at Bonn.

Thus giving himself up freely and without hindrance to the joy and freedom of composing, sustained by the enthusiastic admiration, not merely of his close friends and followers, but by that of the general public, received with warmth wherever the production of his works may lead him, Brahms has now reached that sure pinnacle of success which all true artists may well envy. His works, which now exceed the opus number 100, besides several compositions without opus number, include, as the foregoing biographical sketch shows, every sort of composition with the exception of dramatic works. In number the chamber-music and songs preponderate, while in substance and importance the greater choral and orchestral works hold the most prominent position. It is these latter works which have of late attracted the eyes of the whole musical world towards our artist, and awakened a desire to assign him his place in the development of music. It is now no longer possible to pass over his works as strange and unintelligible; on the contrary, all true lovers of art must feel constrained to range themselves on his side. That it is but a short step from such earnest consideration to admiring acknowledgment, is a truth we have frequently experienced; still, it can hardly be said that anything like a true appreciation of his works and intentions has made its way with the general public. Hence we feel it the more our duty to familiarize ourselves with his works individually and collectively, if we would form a correct judgment upon them. In the biographical sketch we have already called attention to the gulf which separates in so marked a way his earlier works—ops. 1–10—from the succeeding ones. Those who to-day will take a glance at the life and wonderful development of the artist, and then turn back to his early works, will readily understand Schumann's enthusiasm. The independence, the novelty, genius, and poetry that flowed from this distinctly original creative power, the like of which Schumann was ever seeking and striving to foster—in short, all the grand artistic gifts existed here in such surprising abundance, that he might well point to it with the full weight of his authority, confident in its future development. In fact, the novelty and individuality of inspiration, wealth of melody, boldness of design and outline, an almost playful, easy mastery of technique, expression at once impassioned and tender—all these qualities Brahms united in so astonishing a degree, that Schumann's first impression could not have been other than it was. Here we have no rising artist before us, but a perfect master.

Let us consider, for instance, the three great piano-sonatas and the scherzo, which from their great difficulty are unfortunately too little known to the public. We notice at once the solid triumphal opening theme of the first movement of the sonata in C, with its rhythmical resemblance to Beethoven's sonatas, one of which others have already pointed out; let us study the development of this movement, the beautiful contrast between the first and second theme—an effect on which here, as so frequently afterwards, Brahms lavishes his powers—and say if we find anything lacking in originality, expression, or beauty of form. Passing on to the working out of the parts, we ask ourselves at times if the combinations are not too daring, if the harsh harmonies and modulations do not overstep the line of beauty, if the roundness of form is not disturbed by thematic accessories, and science made the first object to the detriment of a natural fundamental development. We gather a similar impression from the other sonatas, that in F sharp minor, which opens in a bold, grandiose style, and reaches a fine climax in the two last movements, while in the first movement the motives are not so interesting: also from the F minor sonata (op. 5), and the trio (op. 8). This last work has been shamefully underrated, and will, it is to be hoped, be better appreciated in future. It also opens in a broad and noble style, and contains in every movement a wealth of beautiful and expressive melody. The scherzo recalls Schubert, and, to our mind, equals him; all the chief characteristics of Brahms' early manner are discernible in this work, especially in the first movement. Let us now turn from the allegro movements, so full of detail, to the melodious adagios, then to the scherzos and trios, where the simple musical phrase, apart from all accessories, attains its highest value, and melodic inspiration is fully displayed. Who can escape the full force of such genius as now reveals itself? It is here that the deep human sympathy and musical inspiration of the poet appear in their fullest perfection.

His language springing from all that is simple, true, and national (Volksmässig), modelled and developed on the highest examples, pours itself out in noble speech, and touches us accordingly. Look at the variations of the first sonata, at the scherzo of the sonata in F sharp minor, with its glorious trio, at the adagio of the sonata in F minor, full of sweet harmonies, of deep inspiration, and again at the scherzo of the trio in B, and we shall truly say that in genuine sentiment, in harmony, and in richness of colouring, Brahms has scarcely ever again equalled these works.

The entirely individual and original character of his imagination, as seen here, gives, as it were, the standard of his future works.

So, too, with the songs of the first period, which in their restricted form and close adherence to the text offer little opportunity for any extravagances of genius. There are three collections whose publication dates from this period: six songs (op. 3) dedicated to Bettina von Arnim, of which the first (*O versenk*) has become one of the most popular; six songs (op. 6) dedicated to Fräulein Japha, which for naturalness, grace, and freshness are distinguished, not only among the earlier, but among the whole of Brahms' works; and, finally, six songs (op. 7) dedicated to Albert Dietrich, especially fine both in conception and execution, and in which the simple stanza-form of the Volkslied is happily employed. If in some of these songs we seem to recognize his early period by the over-bold harmonies and occasional tendency to put expression before melody, the majority of them are so clear, so truly inspired and so pure in form, that it would be difficult to make a distinction between them and his later works. We find throughout all of them an energetic treatment of the general expression, a power of endowing it with a musical unity, a clever way of giving prominence to the most expressive words, at the same time avoiding anything like declamation; and, what is most essential, we find everywhere a clear, concise melody kept independent of the accompaniment in the greatest diversity of character. Brahms often made use of popular forms and chose popular words, producing in these restricted forms the most astonishing effects. Sometimes, again, we recognize in the melodies the influence of the classical period; side by side with Beethoven we especially notice the influence of Franz Schubert, whose well-known, warm, and tender tones Brahms has reproduced so well in his earlier and later compositions. These two composers, and among the old masters we must add Bach, appear throughout as the models under whose influence Brahms' individuality developed itself. At this period we cannot discover either in melody or harmony, in the structure of the movements, or in expression, any direct influence of the new romantic school, especially of Schumann, though this has been so frequently asserted. On the contrary, we are rather disposed to attribute the profound impression which the young artist made upon Schumann to the very fact that their individualities were so distinct; for the great master, with his own strongly marked originality, was by no means blind to his many imitators. We may fairly infer, however, that Brahms, who approached the honoured master with a complete knowledge of his art, fell under his influence, assimilating and profiting by the new impulse in art just so far as was congenial to his nature.

When their friendship ripened, he offered Schumann a flattering homage in the charming, fanciful variations which he composed on a theme from the " Bunte Blätter."

Here, again, it is the narrowness of form which keeps him within bounds, and checks an extravagant play of the imagination. In this charming work, which breathes a poetic fragrance, we notice a distinct progress, and even the daring harmonies occurring here and there are accepted as original and effective. It is in this work also that Brahms has fixed the character of the variation-form which he henceforth adopted, and for which he has always retained a predilection. He does not treat it, like many of the old masters, as a mere rhythmic variation of the air, but seeks after an entirely new creation while retaining the harmony of the theme. Beethoven and Schumann have already shown that this treatment must be adopted if the variation is to keep its position as an independent art-form. In this way a closer relationship is established between the various pieces; they result naturally, as it were, from one another to form a poetic whole. Thus the variations become musical works of art, in the treatment of which Brahms subsequently proved himself a master.

To the first period belong the Ballades (op. 10), four pieces for piano, consisting of a principal movement and an intermezzo, but in their modulations and development more nearly approaching the form of the Rhapsody. Delicate, expressive melody, and surprising effects of harmony, characterize these pieces. The technical details for the piano are excellently treated ; an occasional passage which aims at being too picturesque, and the extreme conciseness of some of the subjects, reveal the early origin of these works. But the idea which inspired them is remarkable. The first, as its title indicates, owes its origin to the Scotch ballad "*Edward,*" and the others were probably prompted by similar ideas. Thus we find him already striving to bridge over the distance between purely instrumental and vocal music, and showing us that he has no need to translate his inspirations into words, for music unaided suffices to express them. After this work comes that pause in his life, as regards publication, which we have already mentioned in the biographical sketch. The early works had, as we know, called forth the most diverse criticisms, which, while they failed to turn aside so gifted a composer from his path, helped to show Brahms' truly artistic nature; for such hints, when just, were seldom lost upon him.

And now begins a time of hard work, of conscientious self-criticism, of unremitting study of the greatest models; henceforth we find him striving after moderation, endeavouring to place himself more in touch with the public, and to conquer all subjectiveness. To arrive at perspicuity and precision of invention, clear design and form, careful elaboration and accurate balancing of effect, now became with him essential and established principles.

So emphatically, indeed, are these principles asserted in the productions of this new period that sometimes intellect seems to outweigh imagination, and a certain harshness of effect takes away from pure enjoyment. It was natural, however, that the reaction which was sure to follow the naïve impulsiveness (Hinausstürmen) of his youth should make itself felt. This is clearly shown in Op. 11, where the composer meets us apparently another man. He is in reality the same. The nature of Brahms' genius is too powerful not to penetrate in all directions, and the further he advances the nobler and more beautiful does his individuality stand out, refined by conscious self-control.

It is impossible henceforth precisely to determine another period, and with an artist still in the plenitude of his power, who may have still further surprises in store for us, it is wiser to abstain from attempting to fix the culminating point of his genius.

But it is of more than passing interest and is surely no fortuitous occurrence, that the first works published after this long interruption, were for orchestra and chorus. First came an orchestral work of great dimensions, but in the old, pleasing and venerable form of a serenade, as Mozart and Beethoven understood it: the Serenade in D for full orchestra (op. 11), which was begun in 1859 and appeared in 1861. The distinguishing features of this composition are simplicity, tenderness, smooth melody; as the title suggests, the heart is charmed and captivated by graceful and joyous tones, free from all passion. This work shows us that severe self-examination, far from interfering with his originality of invention, had, on the contrary, rather elevated it. The first movement, with all its simplicity, is bewitchingly graceful; but the "working out" section does not wholly conceal a certain effort of thought. Some of Brahms' peculiarities are noticeable here, as, for instance, when in the repetition of the theme he lets us hear the minor seventh, recalling the natural modulation, and with it the key of the sub-dominant; very often by this means he has obtained astonishing effects. Again in the formation of the coda, which is independent of the real development, and in many new, unexpected combinations he shows his originality and novelty of conception; the sweet visions momentarily brought before us vanish as in a cloud. Still more highly do we value the first scherzo with its trio, a gem of exquisite melody and chaste detail—modern art can show us few such examples; and we may unquestionably reckon the remaining movements, including the second scherzo (which recalls Beethoven), among the tenderest and most artistic things we possess of that kind. We must not look for an imposing effect, neither had Brahms any such effect in view; but, properly rendered, this work, with its skilful instrumentation, cannot fail to make its mark. The second Serenade in A (op. 16), written in five movements for a small orchestra without violins, possesses the same simple gracefulness, but is more finished in form, while the melodies are even fresher and more lovely. We seem, as so often in Brahms' works, to hear the muse of Schubert re-awakened, but endowed with that fine sense of moderation so often wanting in the works which spring from the over-flowing and unrestrained genius of the impulsive master of Vienna. A wealth of melody is displayed in every movement of this work, but especially in the last, which at once enchants and carries us away; while the second theme brings a calm, sweet as the balmy breath of spring. In the adagio he has happily expressed a tender, dreamy longing. Unfortunately, both Serenades are less well known than they deserve to be.

Side by side with these two works, which are written in a lighter vein, appears one of a very different character which, from the style of the subjects, might be set down to an earlier period, but which, for perfection of form and arrangement, for an unceasing flow of inspiration, unblemished by any over-boldness, undoubtedly belongs to a later date—we mean the Piano concerto in D minor (op. 15).

How different the spirit that pervades this work from the bright and sunny tone of the Serenades. Conceived in a grand style, a vein of sombre passion prevails throughout, which announces itself in the wild, stormy opening. In the first bars the powerful opening theme carries us into the most extended intervals. A grand, almost dramatic development leads us through strong emotion, feverish haste, and deep lamentation, back to calm and hope, when the composer, to express his depth of feeling, enfolds us in all the magic of his harmony. Better still, he knows how to charm us in that wondrous adagio with its luminous melody, and, we may almost say, melting harmonies, while we are fairly carried away by the powerful, rapid finale. Two remarks suggest themselves upon this Concerto, unique in modern musical literature. First, that notwithstanding the brilliance and difficulty of the piano part, there is no tendency towards a display of virtuosity; the pianist has no mere empty, bravura passages to execute at will, but the piano shares with the orchestra the fundamental ideas of the work. Secondly, in all his modulations there is a tone of warmth and penetrating emotion belonging to the third Beethoven period, so dear to all admirers of that master, which Brahms has reproduced in his later works with such particular effect. Whoever wishes to understand him, and inquires into his models, will soon be convinced that he has identified himself with none of the earlier masters so entirely as with Beethoven.

As we have begun, let us continue with the instrumental works of the second period, taking first the chamber-music. In the two sextets for strings (op. 18 in B minor, and op. 36 in G) we observe an increased maturity and independence. The fine individuality constantly reveals itself through severe proportion and perfect form. The theme of the first sextet announces itself with noble dignity—again resembling Beethoven. The movement progresses in pure harmony and beautiful contrasts. A second theme is introduced, as it were in long melodious strides, so ideal, and of such a joyous, hopeful character, that we willingly abandon ourselves to its charm. We must call attention to the thematic development, in which an increased maturity is very noticeable. These developments treated by Mozart, in a short, simple fashion, have become, since Beethoven's time, the arena in which skilful thematic work, and the ingenious transformation and modification of the motives and their constituent parts, have been ever contending in rivalry with each other. Beethoven never looked upon these developments as mere trials of skill, but as a more complete exposition of the emotions to be depicted in his work. It is especially in his great symphonies (the Eroica, for example) that the working and cross-working of the subjects result in a fundamental progress leading to a climax of expression, or conflict; thence we slowly descend to the solution which brings us back to the principal subject. Brahms closely adheres to the example Beethoven laid down; we see how he consciously strives to express himself exactly how and when he wishes, yet always in accordance with the laws of beauty and symmetry. In the B flat sextet he has admirably succeeded in doing this; while in the second sextet we are soon made to forget the storm which suddenly passes over the sunny shores.

Time will not permit us to enumerate all the passages in these two works in which the composer's individuality speaks to us in clear, penetrating accents. Who could resist the warm and striking tones in the coda of the first movement of the B flat sextet, which express so clearly an enthusiastic self-sacrificing devotion for the ideal before him. While his first movement easily reveals itself to the mind of an impartial hearer, that of the G sextet, belonging to a later period, needs a patient and loving study, which will, however, in the highest degree enhance our pleasure in the delicacy and cleverness of its detailed work. The rapid modulations, strange at first hearing, which Brahms so often employs, appear as early as the third bar, where we are taken into the key of E flat, then to B, and back again to G. This tonality recurs with such persistence that it seems to us to express symbolically the thought of home and country. The scanty motives which, in their ingenious transformations and modifications, form the principal phrase, may also appear strange ; but in the tuneful second theme the joy of existence triumphs over doubt and hesitation, and completely carries us away. It is the poet himself who speak here, who reveals to us a thoughtful soul, stirred by visions, ever striving to give expression to his subjective sentiments, and with powerful resolution plunging into the full tide of life—where, indeed, new doubts and trials await him.

But we will not make further attempts at personal interpretation, which is always a hazardous matter. For the slow movements Brahms has employed, in both works, his favourite variation form—and in both cases has treated it with wonderful originality. In the first sextet, the effective theme—a solemn march, moving on majestically in fine harmonies—captivates us at once; in the second, besides the simple theme, with its passages of fourths (Brahms' melody needs only the aid of the simplest harmonies), it is the last variation which, leading from the minor to the major, seems also to lead us from tender lament and gloomy sorrow, to enfold us in a wealth of entrancing melody. The scherzo of the first sextet surprises us by its happy expression of wanton and capricious humour, and shows by its concise form that the extravagance of his early days is completely conquered.

The corresponding movement of the second work is even more original, with its fretful, capricious motives, from which a vigorous waltz theme tries in vain to distract the mind. The finales give a poetic unity to the works; that of the first sextet, by its happy calm and grace, the form of its rondo, the beautiful structure of the melodies, and skilful treatment of the parts, will clearly reveal the example of Beethoven to those who are curious to discover his model; the finale of the second sextet, ingeniously planned, with an expression of energetic will, betrays, to our mind, a little too much effort of intellect.

Space will not allow us to treat fully of his other works; we will therefore only call attention to those which, to our mind, best display the master's individuality. We will select the three quartets for Pf. and strings, of which the first in G minor (op. 25) shows once more, in the first movement, what might be termed a redundance of melodic contents, and a wonderful skill in thematic development; but the climax of melodic charm is reached in the Intermezzo and Trio. We frequently hear Brahms, with whom thought and fancy ever worked together in active union, accused of being obscure. Such an accusation can only come from those who are ignorant of such works as this quartet, above all of its middle movements. Who would not be captivated by the genial Rondo alla Zingarese, with its gay and daring three-bar rhythm? No commonplace mind would have invented that. Here we recognize the Master, who, having drawn from the very fountain-head of national melody, gives it back to the world in all its original purity. In this and the following works the variation no longer serves as a slow movement, but is exchanged for an adagio formed on a melody in the style of a Lied. The sad and plaintive character of the first quartet contrasts with the calmer, brighter tone of the *second in A* (op. 26), which, in the last movement, expresses a wild and wanton gaiety. Here, again, we are surprised at the richness of melodic invention; we are reminded of what Otto Jahn said in praise of Mozart— that just when one expected an end, a new, independent subject, of inimitable charm, would make its appearance. The workmanship of the second surpasses that of the first quartet in elegance and delicacy. This is especially the case with the instrumentation of the first one, in which a heaviness of tone, a strong tendency to orchestral treatment, is noticeable. The third quartet in C minor (op. 60), doubtless belonging to the same period as the others, though only published in later years, rises also to tragic pathos, and reveals, both in technical treatment and invention, an essentially riper development. In the first movement, the deep, sombre, plaintive tones, mingled with ardent passion, show the artist who can at once depict the emotions of the soul and command every secret of his art. The adagio lulls us with blissful and romantic visions, from which we are pitilessly recalled by the feverish agitation of the last movement.

To these works of chamber-music belong the trio for piano, 'cello and horn (op. 40), and the sonata for piano and 'cello in E minor (op. 38). The former is interesting for the happy though unusual combination of instruments by which Brahms does honour to the fine, full tone of the horn. In the first movement he tries a new form by alternating between a meditative, dreamy mood, and a lively movement which strives to chase away the reverie. Beethoven had already tried this in one of his sonatas (op. 54). In the sonata for violoncello the last fugal movement affords in the combination of its three themes a masterpiece of contrapuntal science, which, however, in no way hinders the free display of musical fancy. Brahms attains the perfection in chamber-music in the quintet for piano and strings in F minor (op. 34), which in our opinion surpasses in value all other modern productions of this kind, not excepting Schumann's magnificent quintet. Grandly conceived, deeply pathetic in its expression, rich in inspiration and imagination, it breathes throughout a tone of proud passion and energy, while by its incomparable depth of sentiment and warmth of tone, especially in the adagio, it again recalls Beethoven's later style. The boldness and freedom of the subjects in the first movement (the dimensions of which are so large that they admit the full development of a third theme) have never been surpassed in modern music. The "working-out," the recapitulation of the theme and the coda are masterly. The scherzo, with its combination of several small sections, departing entirely from the customary form, surprises us by its wealth of motives; restlessness, violence, a sense of triumph, possess by turns the troubled mind. The finale, introduced by a slow movement full of emotional tension, errs by being over-charged with subject matter, and appeals more slowly to the understanding. Brahms has also published this work as a sonata for two pianos.

Side by side with these works, and of equally noble origin, though varying in many respects, appear the three string-quartets, the two first in C minor and A minor (op. 51) published many years ago, the third in B flat (op. 67) of recent publication. The string-quartet is justly esteemed the flower of purely instrumental music; here nothing is gained by massive effects, therefore well-turned motives have a good opportunity of showing their real merit by skilful contrasts between somewhat limited individualities; and delicacy of technique is well displayed. Brahms, like a valiant warrior, has striven to follow the example laid down by Beethoven, and reveals to us once more his wealth of melody, his rare skill in form and modulation. The opening movement of the very first quartet is an example of his felicity in evoking colour and emotion; here is every shade of suggestion and description, from gloomy despair to the stormy outbreak of passion, and right onward to the sombre energy of the coda; in the wonderful romance, yearning remembrance unites with heavy oppression; the third movement with its trio in F, plainly revealing the composer's individuality, reminds us of the timid prayer of one who, from afar, sees one faint ray falling from the star of hope; the somewhat scanty finale seems to renew the desperate struggle. In strong contrast to the manly and earnest style of this gloomy, peculiar, but striking tone-picture, is the A minor quartet, with its feminine tenderness and plaintive entreaty. In the first movement of this quartet the principal subject is simply, but cleverly, worked out, while the second theme expresses a deep, touching tenderness. The melodious adagio overflows with hope and resignation, and breathes a tone of earnest meditation broken by an outburst of quick, pulsating vitality—an episode in the scherzo; the last movement is full of energy and newly acquired confidence: so that a searching inquiry into the spirit of the work will disclose the four movements joined in a poetic unity. The same idea may be also followed out in the third and last quartet. Written in a lighter and livelier vein, full of imagination, delicate in detail, it still is not without traces of certain affectations of obscurity. In the first movement the rhythm resulting from the combination of various sorts of time surprises us. The adagio is all reverie and sweet harmony; the dance-rhythms of the third movement interest us in a strange, fantastic way; above all, the lovely and ingenious variations which serve as a finale, whose concise theme is a masterpiece of conception and modulation, recall a more peaceful mood.

The last few years have brought us yet another graceful piece of chamber-music, the sonata for piano and violin in G (op. 78). The sweet and noble subjects of the first movement, in broad $\frac{6}{4}$ time, lull us into a blissful calm far from any shadow of gloom. The adagio has a graver tone; and the last movement, for which Brahms employs the significant theme of one of his earlier songs (*Regenlied* op. 59), seems to tell us that the former state of bliss has passed and can exist no more save in memory, that we must bid it farewell and turn to stern endeavour and ideal aspirations.

We have now reached the last and greatest of Brahms' instrumental compositions—the orchestral works. The Serenades had already paved the way for such, but it was only in later years that Brahms returned to orchestral composition. He begins with a fine original work: the "Variations for Orchestra on a theme by Haydn" (op. 56), which is originally the andante of a divertimento for wind instruments; the variations were written in the summer of 1873 at Tutzing on the Starnberger See, and first performed in Vienna on November 2nd in the same year. Haydn and Beethoven, as we know, had already written variations for orchestra in symphonies, but this was the first time they appeared separately. Brahms was probably taken by the peculiar five-bar rhythm of this charming theme.

In accordance with the method already alluded to, each variation is an independent tone-picture, in which the orchestral colouring is excellently employed. The frequent use of the minor key is characteristic. Among the technical features we are especially interested by the bass figure with its constant renewal. Each instrument takes it up in turn, while every variety of motive and florid figure join in this festive cortége, which, with its brilliancy strangely enhanced by triangle and piccolo, leads on to the peroration and dies away with the close of the piece.

By means of the two symphonies, which have brilliantly fulfilled the long hopes of his admirers, Brahms has won his place in Beethoven's domain of art.

He has shown that it avails nothing to break through form, which was never desired by Beethoven—(for whom, in his later years, notwithstanding the 9th symphony, purely instrumental music was amply sufficient)—but that it is all important to endow form with an independent individuality. To understand and feel this, however, Brahms' works, like those of all true artists, need a patient and devoted study.

The first symphony in C minor (op. 68), strikes a highly pathetic chord. As a rule, Brahms begins simply and clearly, and gradually reveals more difficult problems; but here he receives us with a succession of harsh discords, the picture of a troubled soul gazing longingly into vacancy, striving to catch a glimpse of an impossible peace, and growing slowly, hopelessly resigned to its inevitable fate. In the first movement we have a short, essentially harmonious theme, which first appears in the slow movement, and again as the principal theme of the allegro. At first this theme appears unusually simple, but soon we discover how deep and impressive is its meaning when we observe how it predominates everywhere, and makes its energetic influence felt throughout. We are still more surprised when we recognize in the second theme, so full of hopeful aspiration, with its chromatic progression, a motive which has already preceded and introduced the principal theme, and accompanied it in the bass; and when the principal theme itself re-appears in the bass as an accompaniment to the second theme, we observe, in spite of the complicated execution and the psychic development, a simplicity of conception and creative force which is surprising. The development is carried out quite logically and with wonderful skill, the recapitulation of the theme is powerful and fine, the coda is developed with ever-increasing power; we feel involuntarily that a strong will rules here, able to cope with any adverse circumstances which may arise. In this movement the frequent use of chromatic progressions and their resultant harmonies is noticeable, and shows that Brahms, with all his artistic severity, employs, when needful, every means of expression which musical art can lend him. Inversion and augmentation of the themes take place frequently and with ease. The melodious adagio, with its simple opening, a vein of deep sentiment running throughout, is full of romance; the colouring of the latest Beethoven period is employed by a master hand. To this movement succeeds the naïve grace of an allegretto, in which we are again surprised at the variety obtained by the simple inversion of a theme. The last movement, the climax of the work, is introduced by a solemn adagio of highly tragic expression. After a long pause, the horn is heard, with the major third, giving forth the signal for the conflict, and now the allegro comes in with its truly grand theme. This closing movement, supported by all the power and splendour of the orchestra, depicts the conflict, with its moment of doubt, its hope of victory, and moves on before us like a grand triumphal procession. To this symphony, which might well be called heroic, the second symphony (op. 73 in *D*.) bears the same relation that a graceful, lightly-woven fairy-tale bears to a great epic poem. Everything breathes a joyous calm, a peaceful existence without conflict or discord, though not entirely free from desires or forebodings. Gay and gladsome sounds the horn, in the opening bars, calling us so brightly to the enjoyment of happy hours, that soon all join in the gaiety and unite in a festive strain. The adagio, in B major, interests us in a stranger fashion; first comes a short introduction consisting of a melodic motive given out by the cello, then from the wind instruments a distant foreboding call, to which the cantilena trembling, and ever recommencing, seems to be listening in fear. We believe that in this strange, original movement, whose fine sonority and variety of rhythms are impregnated with a legendary spirit (Märchenduft), the composer has intentionally striven to express the hesitation and fearfulness experienced on beholding a weird apparition, which still irresistibly entices and beckons us onward. The mind is recalled from this vision to the reality of life by a bright and rustic waltz theme, but the two episodes, free variations on the theme, again excite a momentary trouble; the heart is still oppressed and not yet free to abandon itself to gaiety. It is only in the brilliant finale that the full joy of life takes possession of it once more.

In these two—so far the greatest—of our composer's instrumental works, we shall certainly find plenty of material in which to study Brahms' art from a technical point of view. Here, however, it only concerns us to give a general impression of them as far as our limited space will allow. The violin concerto (op. 77) may also be included among the great orchestral works, being closely allied in tonality and in character to the second symphony. Although the violin part presents throughout the utmost difficulties of execution, yet its first duty is to interpret the composer's poetical intention. This work was written for Joachim.

The compositions for piano, his own

particular instrument, keep pace with the orchestral works, though they are not so numerous as might have been expected from his first attempts in this direction. Brahms has written no more piano sonatas since the three belonging to his early period; he applies himself by preference to the more restricted forms, such as the variation, and single piano pieces under various titles. We have already called attention to the distinctive position he assigned to the *variation*, by making it an independent invention, having for its basis the original harmony of the theme. By the way in which he grouped the variations, giving the individual pieces a closer relationship, and endowing them with an artistic unity of expression. Thus the two books which appeared as Op. 21 (variations on a theme of his own, and on a Hungarian theme), are distinctly original works. The first are remarkable for that enchanting warmth of colouring peculiar to Brahms' harmony; the melodious theme is much enhanced in expression by its varied rhythm (sometimes four, sometimes five bars), while in the second variations the time of the theme alternates between $\frac{3}{4}$ and $\frac{4}{4}$. No intelligent hearer will take offence at these innovations, which are interesting and effective because of their originality, nor seek to judge them by ordinary rules. Brahms gives a proof of his contrapuntal skill in the fifth variation of the first book, which is treated as a canon in contrary motion. In the second book the sudden change from major to minor has a surprising effect, and we are still more struck by the curious—we may call it Hungarian—colouring.

The variations on a theme by Handel (op. 24), take even a higher place. We have seen them justly described somewhere as the *chef d'œuvre* of modern piano music. The wonderful wealth of inventive power displayed in every individual number (there are twenty-five) is crowned at last by a genial and freely handled fugue, whose subject seems to grow spontaneously out of Handel's theme; in brilliance and variety this movement is hardly surpassed in modern music. Interesting in another way, but equally perfect, are the variations for four hands (op. 23) on a theme of Schumann's—that same theme which the master in his last wanderings fancied Schubert himself had brought to him. Knowing this fact, no one in looking through the variations could fail to be touched by the deep sympathy for the honoured master which inspires this work. The variation-form is used here to express the purest and noblest poetry. The whole work is full of it, but especially that particular passage (variation 4), where the grief caused by an irreparable loss is followed by a noble, ideal aspiration—the joyful hope that from these ashes may spring a new life. The funeral march at the close of the work with which the theme is united, produces a profound impression. Yet these works are only known to a few!

Brahms' last variations for piano, on a theme of Paganini's (they are published in two separate books, and were played by him in Vienna at the beginning of 1867), are the finest and most beautiful as regards the employment of technical resources. As their second title "*Studies for Piano*" indicates, they are equally intended to serve for the purpose of instruction, and indeed can only be played by a pianist possessing the finest execution. They afford a good example of the way in which Brahms has enriched the technique of the pianoforte—a subject, however, which we do not intend to enter upon here. Extended passages, harmonic progressions, the combination of various movements, the clever concealment of the melody under emotional figures, polyphony applied to the piano—these, the chief features of Brahms' technique, produce, in these variations, many new and astonishing effects; while at the same time we are captivated and carried away by the fantastic, fleeting, melodic pictures, which one and the same simple theme brings before us, all of which are filled with deep earnestness and powerful energy.

These great works are followed, by way of diversion as it were, by a series of lighter compositions in which his melodic invention is still more brilliantly displayed. Who does not admire the Waltzes for four hands (op. 39)? What an inexhaustible wealth of pure melody; what art in the harmonic structure; what clever employment of this small unpretentious form for the production of charming effects, now tender and dreamy, now proud and bold, now wildly fantastic, now serious and melancholy! A master of the art of melody speaks in these works; to them we may apply these words quoted elsewhere: "He who passes carelessly by such blossoms as these, was never created to enjoy music."

The Hungarian Dances have become still more popular; they are national melodies by Hungarian composers, which Brahms, with his perfect knowledge of the instrument, has invested with every advantage of modern piano-technique, while retaining all their fantastic charm.[1] The authorship of these dances has given rise to a very idle controversy, which ended in an attack upon the com-

---

[1] The composers of the original melodies are named in the "Allgemeine Musikalische Zeitung," 1874, p. 348.

poser. Those who started the subject did not, or would not, see that the work has no opus number, and bears distinctly upon the title page the words—"Arranged by J. Brahms." The first books have been followed by two others which also reveal wonderful originality and knowledge. Brahms has arranged the first set of dances for orchestra.

Of late he has returned to a grander style of piano compositions. The eight Piano-pieces (op. 76) show all the characteristics of his style in their greatest intensity, both as regards imagination and workmanship. Among them are some which, by their simplicity and natural sentiment, captivate at once both ear and heart; they are those entitled "*Intermezzi*," especially No. 3, which displays all the magic of modern harmony. The others called "*Capriccios*" are most difficult to hearer and performer, but the invention is even more remarkable. In these compositions, by means of the modifications of the themes and figures, by doubling the value of the notes, and by the combination of various sorts of rhythms, Brahms shows an almost playful command of rhythmical and contrapuntal skill. We think the second piece in B minor the best of the collection.

We hesitate to pass a decisive judgment upon the two Rhapsodies for piano (op. 79) which have lately appeared. The title leads us to expect a free, ballad-like form, and the variety of motives confirms the expectation; but there is no trace of a desire to break through rules, the form is severe and well marked. Their chief characteristic is a harsh severity, that of the second an almost gloomy seriousness; but both pieces are remarkable in inspiration and execution. We have often dwelt upon Brahms' skill in counterpoint, the value of which is well shown in the instrumental works, but we must mention one composition, which, though little known, is perhaps the most perfect example of his skill in uniting the severity of the old school to the greatest warmth of sentiment. We mean the Organ Fugue which was published in 1884 as the supplement of the "Allgemeine Musikalische Zeitung" (No. 29). The simple theme is at once reversed in the second part (as answer); the subordinate parts are treated in the same way; and later on, the same device is employed in the case of a chromatic theme which makes its appearance. Thus, observing the strictest technical rules, while the profound contemplative character of the composition attains intense expression, Brahms creates a work of art which leaves us no doubt of the ease with which he would overcome all similar tasks. That should be especially proved by the vocal music.

Schumann's prophecy that the young artist would win laurels as soon as he turned to orchestral and choral composition, has now been more than fulfilled. His first works in this style, which have led him on step by step to the climax, date from the period when he reappeared, matured and refined by study and self-criticism. Many of these works may be considered as studies in the sacred style; they show the genius and the iron will with which he mastered the severest forms of this style, and a determination to gain an absolute command over every branch of his art. They also show, what often escapes notice, that his greatest creation in this sphere, the German Requiem, had many precursors, and is the result of a natural development. We call attention to the fact that the majority of these small sacred works are not intended to be sung at divine service, but simply meant to render in an artistic form the sentiments evoked by the words.

In this respect the *Ave Maria* (op. 12), for female voices and orchestra, is particularly distinguished by sweetness and truth of sentiment. The uninterrupted sequence of thirds, with all its harmonic science, gives an artless impression, and seems to indicate a popular melody idealised. Taken as a whole, it is the expression of humble, heartfelt supplication, of complete abandonment to a Being to whom one draws near in prayer.

The Funeral Hymn (op. 13) for chorus and wind instruments, to words beginning, "Nun lasst uns den Leib begraben," is more serious and important. The harmony is simple, yet grand; the expression of profound sorrow, the transition to calm and hope, all these feelings, expressed by simple means in noble symmetry, make this work the true forerunner of the Requiem.

The "Marienlieder" (op. 22), which can hardly be considered as a sacred work, consist of a number of old German songs relating to the worship of the Virgin. They are treated in an old-fashioned way, recalling Eccard and his times. The melodies are adapted as far as possible to the expression and rhythm of the words, every reminiscence of modern melody is avoided, and though the harmonic treatment is severely simple, consisting as far as possible in the use of the triad, still the composer moves with grace and skill within his self-imposed limits. The pearl of the collection is "*Maria's Kirchgang.*"

The next work of this sort, the 13*th* Psalm ("How long wilt Thou forget me, O Lord?" op. 27), for three-part female chorus with organ, may really be termed sacred music. The composer may even have had in his mind some idea of a church performance. We observe a sober restraint, and the complete renunciation of the rich resources to which Mendelssohn had recourse in his setting of the psalms. With all possible simplicity, Brahms expresses the idea of an imploring multitude filled with the sense of abandonment and helplessness. Through the austerity of the old church-style we feel that warmth of tone so characteristic of Brahms.

In the two motets for five voices *a capella* (op. 29), we find Brahms adopting the Bach school of polyphonic art. Here in every direction we meet with fugal science, with canons, with inversions and working out of the subject. In the intrinsic value of the motives, in the expression of the words, and in the modulations, the composer is quite himself, and we cannot hint at mere imitation.

We pass the same judgment upon the Sacred Song by Paul Flemming (op. 30), for four voices, mixed chorus and organ or piano. The voices work out a double canon to an independent accompaniment, which seems to elevate and elucidate the sentiment of tender confidence produced by such simple means.

He is still more austere in the three sacred choruses to Latin words, for women's voices without accompaniment (op. 37). Rendered well and correctly, these choruses would give an effect resembling Palestrina's manner; as Brahms' compositions, we may class them as studies in the old style. Of late he has again proved how much this style attracts him by the two motets (op. 74), which are the best things he has accomplished in this branch. In them he has succeeded admirably in endowing the old forms with the modern spirit. Let us turn from these smaller works to the German Requiem (op. 45), to which we must devote the more attention as it is generally acknowledged to be the work which has given Brahms his present position in the musical world. As we have already mentioned, it was partially performed in 1867, and a full performance followed in 1868. The origin of such a work in the composer's soul is concealed from us. He alone can say if the impulse was due to personal experiences. Suffice it to say that the chosen subject so entirely filled his inmost being, that it gave him a complete mastery over his art. The originality of his treatment is shown at once by the title, *German Requiem*. To those who cling to the letter of the word it is hardly a correct title, since "Requiem," strictly speaking, means the Latin mass for the dead. Brahms, in order to secure a greater freedom of musical treatment, has given the word a more general meaning (we recall the Requiem for Mignon). In the Latin Requiem the words themselves, with the constant recurrence of the *Dies iræ*, seem to determine the character of the work—a solemnity, a profound grief, lamentation over the vanity of all things human, finally the expectation of death and judgment. These characteristics prevail in Mozart's Requiem, still more in Cherubini's; and modern writers such as Schumann and F. Kiel, who have composed similar works, even where they have succeeded in introducing a milder and more subjective tone, have still been fettered by the words. Unlike them, Brahms has arranged his own text. Selecting from the Bible a number of passages relating to death and eternity, he has so bound them together as to form perfectly connected musical phrases, the combination of which lends itself to produce well-marked contrasts and variety of character. The Requiem preserves its fundamental conception, and its fullest, intensest expression; while by contrasting with its solemn tone, either in the same number or in the following one, a picture of consolation and hope, of resignation, thankfulness or praise, a calmer spirit, a sense of atonement is given to the funeral music of the German Requiem.

The work is divided into seven distinct parts for chorus and orchestra; in numbers three and six a baritone solo, and in number five a soprano solo, is introduced. The characteristic of the first chorus is deep, sorrowful lamentation (Matthew v., " Blessed are they that mourn "), interrupted by a striking expression of hope (Psalm cxxvi., " They that sow in tears shall reap in joy "). The second chorus is more elaborate; the chorus joins in unison to the solemn music of a funeral march, moving onward like a sombre fate (1 Peter i. 24, " For all flesh is as grass "). A second, softer phrase breaks in (James, v. 7, " Be patient therefore "), and leads by a short transition to the final chorus, which is a fugue (Isaiah xxxv., " And the redeemed of the Lord shall return "). In the third chorus the solo expresses in anxious and emotional tones the vanity of human life (Psalm xxxix., " Lord, make me to know the measure of my days "). This is then taken up and worked out by the chorus, the sentiment grows resigned and humble (" Surely all my days here are as an hand-breadth "). Supplication and doubt are expressed in turn, and finally give place to firm and trustful hope (" But the righteous souls are in the hand of God "). The last words are developed upon an uninterrupted pedal-point into a grand fugue, which appears to have been a stumbling-block to many critics of the Requiem. Heard, as the composer meant it to be, with a large chorus and a proportionate number of instruments, we cannot fail to find, besides consummate contrapuntal skill, the expression of firm trust most wonderfully rendered. The fourth number ("How lovely is thy dwelling place, O Lord") calms us once more by its gentle seriousness and tender grace, while the dignity of the subject is never for a moment forgotten; under a delicate web true artistic treasures lie concealed. The fifth chorus carries the hearer to ideal heights. While a high voice proclaims the consolation to follow present sorrow ("Ye now are sorrowful, howbeit ye shall again behold Me"), the chorus answer simply and touchingly "Yea, I will comfort you, as one whom his own mother comforteth."

The sixth chorus is the climax of the work. Opening in uneasy, expectant tones ("Here on earth have we no continuing place"), we presently hear the soloist proclaiming the promise of the

Resurrection ("Lo, I unfold to you a mystery"); and now the chorus with deep foreboding repeats the prophecy, and the expression gradually works up to an outburst of wild energy ("For the trumpet shall sound;" "O death, where is thy sting?"). Then, when the storm of feeling is at its height and nothing further can be expected, the master-hand puts forth its power; a sudden change of rhythm, of tone-colour, of tempo, and we have arrived at that climax of the development which, in spite of all that has gone before, only leads up to the glorious outburst, "Worthy art Thou to be praised, Lord of honour and might." The hymn of praise which follows—a brilliant double fugue—was hardly a suitable ending to the funeral music; the composer, therefore, returns in the last chorus to a tone of mourning, in which bitter and inconsolable grief gives way to more hopeful thoughts ("Blessed are the dead which die in the Lord," Revelation iv. 13). The subject of the first chorus is heard once more with the soft and solemn tone of the harp, and the movement comes to an end in a sentiment of pardon and peace recalling to our minds the fundamental idea of the work.

The Requiem not only points to the climax of Brahms' power; it remains also a monument of serious, lasting art, of eloquent expression and consummate technical skill. In these days when in art, as in other things, the world looks by preference for superficial, easy-going enjoyment, we turn with special satisfaction to such a work as this, confident that here, if anywhere, the tradition of the good old classical days is kept alive. But the study of this work will help from the very beginning to make us appreciate the composer's individuality; for here we see the austerity and seriousness of the old school associated in a logical union with all the warmth of feeling and enlarged psychological expression of modern art.

A few years later, Brahms followed up this work by another choral work, also due in part to the same lofty inspiration, the *Triumphlied* (op. 55, dedicated to the Emperor William), with words from the Revelation, arranged for eight-part chorus and full orchestra. It is divided into three broadly planned choral movements, and for its grand scale and musical science almost surpasses the Requiem. The art of Bach and Handel seems to have risen again in modern guise. "Hallelujah, Heil und Preis" (Hallelujah, praise the Lord), runs the first chorus, and in the independent, skilfully elaborated theme we recognize the well-known tune of the Prussian hymn "Heil dir im Siegerkranz," though it is here transformed by all the lustre of polyphonic art. A second chorus, equally fine, but more moderate in tempo, leads up to the hymn of praise. This starts in stirring figures, "For the Omnipotent God hath exalted His kingdom," and continues till the words "O be joyful, let all be glad," with melodious, graceful changes and surprising modulations, while in the meantime the bass gives out the chorale, "Now thank we all our God." Then follows a baritone solo full of enthusiasm for the victorious hero, the chorus celebrates once more in powerful tones the overthrow of the enemy, and sings with ever increasing brilliancy the hallelujah of victory. It is with joy and pride that we see the greatest composer of the day joining the art of music to the history of our own times in an inseparable union.

Brahms has produced another great vocal work in the cantata *Rinaldo*, for tenor solo, male chorus and orchestra (op. 50). This poem of Goethe's, which seems peculiarly adapted for musical treatment, is derived from an episode in Tasso's "Jerusalem Delivered." The brave Rinaldo, entangled in Armida's magic toils, lingers by her in unmanly self-forgetfulness and is delivered by two knights. They hold before him an adamantine shield, in which he sees his own reflection, and, filled with shame and indignation, he tears himself from Armida's side in spite of her lamentations. As he sails away she exercises once more her magic arts, but in vain. Then giving herself up to a frenzy of grief, she invokes a terrific storm, and her palace, with all its magnificence, is utterly destroyed. Goethe has given a higher meaning to this episode, for instead of making Rinaldo the mere puppet of a mechanical enchantment and disenchantment, he makes him a young man possessed of emotions, human and sensitive, who, when the envoys arrive (represented in Goethe's poem by a chorus of knights) and show him his degenerate image, at once recognizes his duty, but is torn between that duty and his love : he is by no means insensible to Armida's tears, and, gazing on the scene of destruction, departs with a stricken heart. In this human truth lies the germ, the form and character of a musical work, and it is not surprising that it should have attracted Brahms and that he should have handled it so successfully. With warm and life-like colours he depicts the youth, glowing with love, his laments, his despair and final resignation. In striking contrast he represents the two knights; we seem to see them first busily preparing for their departure (here he makes a wonderfully characteristic picture out of a few of Goethe's words), then fulfilling their mission, not coldly or mechanically, but as sympathetic friends who do their duty with wisdom and forbearance. It is this that lends to the choruses that feature of gentleness and sometimes even of solemnity. We draw attention to the tact with which Brahms has treated the situation where the shield is held up before the youth ; it is not descriptive music, but rather the expression of sudden fear, of complete fascination, emotions which easily lend themselves to musical representation. Musically speaking, the last movement, representing in bright figures the joyous and hopeful emotions of the travellers' return, is even more remarkable.

Besides these great choral works, we find several minor ones, of which the " Schicksalslied " (" Song of Fate," op. 54) from Hölderlin's *Hyperion* is remarkable for seriousness and truthful sentiment. The contrast between the calm, untroubled existence of the Olympian spirits and man's restless life, ever tormented by indefinite desires, is depicted in two characteristic choral movements; but it is especially the longing after a purer and higher existence which is exquisitely expressed in the orchestral introduction and finale.

The Rhapsody (Fragment from Goethe's *Harzreise im Winter*, op. 53) for alto-solo, male chorus and orchestra, is of a more sombre tone, more abstruse, and demanding careful study. The gloomy and misanthropical mood of a wretched being, cut off from his fellow-men, is truly and strikingly depicted, and the alto voice mingling with the chorus admirably expresses a tone of gentle supplication. But the sombre, strange harmonies, the occurrence of unusual intervals, the conflicting rhythm—alternating between $\frac{6}{4}$ and $\frac{3}{2}$—make this work, so perfect in form, somewhat incomprehensible at first hearing. This is, however, to be expected in all the more serious works of art. Joh. Fr. Reichardt had already chosen this poem as the subject of a musical composition; so that any one who feels inclined may easily compare the Past with the Present.

Brahms has united a number of short choral works into various collections. He has frequently employed women's voices with wonderful effect, as in the Four Songs (op. 17), with accompaniment for two horns and harp, among which Eichendorff's "*Wohin ich geh' und schaue*" is distinguished by beauty of melody and rhythm; also in the Twelve Songs and Romances, with optional pianoforte accompaniment (op. 44, in two books). These are delicate pictures of exquisite finish. They have been compared to "flowers gathered in wandering on the mountains, breathing a fragrance as of Nature herself, who has produced them." Brahms has published a book of Songs for male chorus (op. 41), mostly of a martial character; the most remarkable of these is the old German ballad, "*Ich schwing mein Horn ins Jammerthal*," arranged in the severest progression of triads; it has also been published as a solo.

The Three Songs for six-part chorus (op. 62) are full of charm, especially the second (*Vineta*) which strikes us as well by its pleasing harmony as by the delicate treatment of the five-bar rhythm; while in Ossian's *Darthula's Grabgesang* the curious tone-colouring cannot fail to interest us.

In the Seven Songs for mixed chorus (op. 62) the polyphonic treatment reasserts itself, and aided by the resources of modern harmony, Brahms creates, to popular words, characteristic and truthful tone-pictures. In this series we would especially mention the "Deutsches Volkslieder." This collection consists of old tunes, religious and secular, taken from Meister, Kretzschmer, and Zuccalmaglio, which Brahms has arranged for four voices, sometimes with polyphonic treatment, sometimes with the simplest harmony, but always with modulations suitable to the words; they are dedicated to the Vienna Singakademie.

Lastly, must we not consider that copious stream of genuine music which seems to flow in inexhaustible abundance through the Songs? In every branch of his art we have found Brahms creating with the ease of a master-hand; but when we turn to the songs with piano accompaniment, we begin to doubt whether it is not here that he is at his greatest.

His abundance of unborrowed and beautiful melodies, intelligible and effective, even without the aid of accompaniments, admirably fit him to be a composer of songs, as also his poetic tact, his feeling for what is natural and true, and his wonderful skill in the treatment of form. In the present day a marked distinction is drawn between the popular ballad (Volkslied) of simple stanza form, in which the same melody serves to express the greatest variety of ideas, and the "durchkomponirtes Lied,"[1] which admits of a more extended development of the expression. Brahms' compositions cannot be distinctly placed in either category, for he is equally skilful in his treatment of both kind of songs. From his earliest works he has shown a feeling after that truthfulness to nature which is the characteristic of popular and national music ; thus many of his songs have in their style of melody, or in form, a direct, popular origin. But starting from this basis, he gradually works his way up to more elaborate songs, to romances, to

[1] A song having different music for every stanza.

grand scenas, regardless of the category under which his works may be placed, his first object being to clothe his text with suitable musical forms and sentiments. If he recalls Schubert in abundance and charm of melody, Schumann in delicacy and truth of detail, and Franz in neatness of elaboration, he cannot be looked upon as an imitator of any of these composers; he is still independent and original while employing all the artistic resources of his predecessors.

We especially call attention to the good taste which has invariably guided him in the choice of words. Entertaining a rooted dislike to all empty phrases, he demands poetry of sterling value that vibrates in the heart; and he seeks it not only in popular material (*Des Knaben Wunderhorn* supplied him with a wealth of subjects), but in the great classic poets and their successors, Goethe, Hölty, Tieck, Simrock, Kopisch, Platen,

Schenkendorf, Kl. Groth, and Mörike. He also shows a liking for the poetry of other nations, the taste for which was introduced by Daumer, Heyse, etc. The character of the accompaniment is always appropriate to the words. In the simple songs, resembling the Volkslied, it is naturally kept in the background; but if sentiments more complete and subjective are to be expressed with greater elaboration, the accompaniment must needs become a more independent and integral part of the composition. Brahms knows how to seize in a masterly way the distinctive colouring and character of his subject, and to fix them by clear motives and decisive rhythms; thus he obtains a unity of idea, whether the song appears as a finished melody—which is the general rule—or soars as melodic declamation above the accompaniment. Brahms makes use of some of Schubert's peculiarities in song writing, as, for instance, when he puts the voice part a third below the accompaniment. It is in the songs above all that we find that tone of heartfelt warmth which, enhanced by a wonderful harmonic colouring, touches us so deeply.

It would be very interesting to follow out these general remarks by a study of the songs in detail ; but space will only allow us briefly to enumerate the various collections. One important series, the Songs and Romances (op. 14), mark that first period of strengthened and refined creative power. The touching melodies and popular character of this collection distinguish it from all the others ; but it is more especially in the sonnet, "*Ach könnt' ich, könnte vergessen sie,*" that we find a profound emotional sentiment expressed in captivating melody. The Five Poems (op. 19) follow next, among which Mörike's "*An eine Aeolsharfe*" charms by its original harmony and fervent expression. The Nine Songs, with words by Platen and Daumer, are even more delicately finished, but demand a more cultivated audience. One of them, "*Wie bist du meine Königin*," full of beautiful feeling, has become more generally known.

Brahms attains the perfection of his lyric art in the Romances from Tieck's *Magelone* (op. 33, in five books). We cannot pass them by without a few words. Tieck's romance, of which these poems form a part, depicts an inner life so intense, so changeful, as to exclude the simple Lied-form, and Brahms has had recourse to longer movements, with intermezzi, or to combining several parts into a whole. The first song, in which the stirring life of the knight is portrayed as in a grand picture, must be noticed as illustrating how unity of form may be preserved while expressing the greatest variety of feeling. But all these songs, whether they depict the awakening of love ("*Sind es Schmerzen, sind es Freuden*"), the anxious forebodings which disturb joy and happiness ("*schlage, sehnsüchtige Gewalt*"), the pain of separation, or the expectation of a new happiness ("*wie frisch und froh mein Sinn sich hebt*"), reveal throughout a profound power of expression which manifests itself in an absolutely novel way. This, however, can only be understood by a diligent study of the works themselves.

Equally fine are the Four Songs (op. 43). Take, for instance, the Wendish Volkslied, "*von ewiger Liebe*"; has music ever given us so deep an insight into the inward feelings of a troubled heart? Or have the rhythmic proportion and harmonious charm of Hölty's "*Mainacht*" ever been surpassed, or even equalled, in the present day? To the same period belongs the wonderful collection of Songs published by Simrock (op. 46–49), and consisting of four books ; among these the *Botschaft*, after Hafiz ("*Wehe Lüftchen*"), and the Magyar song, "*Sah dem edlen Bildnis*," are remarkable for artistic handling. A few songs of a more popular character, or treated in a simple, ballad-like form, are more taking to the ear, such as the dainty little *Wiegenlied*, with its independent, delicate accompaniment, which has become very popular. The simplicity with which Brahms treats Goethe's poems (there are two in this collection) seems a further proof of his artistic tact. Goethe's lyric art is so perfect, so self-contained, that its effect can hardly be enhanced by music; Brahms therefore leaves it to produce its own effect in its original form, and only drapes it with music as with a suitable garment. By this means the rhythm is clearly defined, and any change of character delicately indicated by the modulations and closing of the periods. Elsewhere, however, we find Goethe's words treated with greater freedom.

The six books (op. 57, 58, and 59) form another series, all of which are written and selected with great taste; some will only appeal to a cultivated audience; others, expressively rendered, will give immediate pleasure. Here the popular style is not prominent. We mention as most remarkable the *Perlenschnurr*, the "*Willkommen, holde Sommernacht,*" impregnated with delicious harmony; Goethe's "*Dämmrung senkte sich von oben,*" characteristically treated; and finally, the wonderful *Regenlied* (Kl. Groth), a song full of reminiscences of happy youth, the theme of which again appears in the Violin Sonata.

This collection is followed by the " Lieder und Gesänge " (op. 63), all remarkable for construction, deep expression, and clever accompaniments; the best known of them is, perhaps, the first one, "*Meine Liebe ist grün wie der Fliederbusch,*" which is full of spirit. The five books (op. 69-72), lately published, are a wonderful collection, among which, besides popular words, Brahms has set some of the poems of the Alsatian, Karl Candidus. In these last songs he seems to approach a more decidedly classical form and clearer elucidation of the subject. Taking one at random— "*Der Liebsten Schwur,*" for instance—we do not hesitate to reckon it one of the best compositions of its kind. Again and again it reminds us of Franz Schubert, whose wealth of melody lives once more in Brahms; while the latter surpasses him in conciseness of form and exact workmanship.

A collection published by Luckhardt of Cassel contains another song, Eichendorff's '*Mondnacht,*' which is a striking example of the essentially distinct individualities of Brahms and Schumann.

Besides the Lieder, Brahms has published a series of compositions for several voices. First come a great number of duets—three Duets, op. 19; four Duets for alto and baritone, op. 28; Duets for soprano and contralto, op. 61 and 66; and lastly, the ballads and romances for two voices, op. 75. One and all display the peculiarities of Brahms' style, but they vary considerably in form. Sometimes the voices keep, as it were, parallel, sometimes they alternate, or different characters form little scenes as in the ballads of the *Knight and the Nun* (op. 28), and *Edward* (op. 75), which are inventions full of genius, skilfully carried out. Again we would call attention, as an example of his simpler style, to the "*Hüt du Dich*" (op. 66), in which we recognize the tone of tenderness and naïveté which characterizes all the songs of his later period.

Both collections of quartets with piano accompaniment (op. 31 and 64) show the same variety of treatment, whether a homophonic form prevails, or whether the arrangement of the parts results in little dramatic pictures. This latter style affords excellent opportunity for delicate contrasts and skilful musical structure; but the quartets treated in the first manner are more original, more effective in melody and harmony. Among them "*Der Gang zum Liebchen*" (op. 31) and "*Der Abend*" (op. 64) are the most noticeable, especially the latter, which is a setting of Schiller's "*Senke, strahlender Gott.*" This is a masterly composition. The musical motives are admirably adapted to the poetical rhythm, the profound idea of the poem is intelligently rendered, the whole carried out in fine symmetry and with beautiful harmony.

We should like to mention another work which, for wealth of melody, charm of expression, and perfection of form, has scarcely been equalled even by Brahms; we mean the "Liebeslieder" and the "Neue Liebeslieder" (op. 52 and 65), waltzes for four hands and voices. These are in the simplest Lied-form, of varied time and rhythm; the short words are mostly taken from Daumer's "Polydora." The idea may seem strange at first; and yet the custom of singing to dance-music is as old as the enjoyment of song and merry-making itself. (Among the songs with piano accompaniment, too, there are several which intentionally adopt a dance-rhythm.) In these little musical pictures, the dance, which is the first idea musically and instrumentally, remains independent; and in this respect they resemble the first waltzes for four hands. To this the voice parts are joined *ad libitum;* but instead of merely following the melody for piano, they introduce, though in concordant harmony, individual motives, thus producing a charming general effect, in which the original conception is hardly recognizable, and we ask in vain if the melody is made for the words, or the words for the melody. What modern composition affords such a wealth of noble, graceful motives? Take, for instance, the waltzes, "*Am Donaustrande,*" "*Vögelein durchrauscht die Luft,*" "*Es bebet das Gesträuche,*" where can we find anything like them in the present day? The words, which all contain some delicate love-story, are sometimes bright and gay, sometimes grave, sad, and passionate. Who can help being captivated, for instance, by the playfully ill-humoured "*Nein, es ist nicht anzukommen*"? Towards the end of the second set, the Master rises with rare art and grandeur above the playful mood. Adopting Goethe's words, "*Nun, ihr Musen, genug,*" he works them out in a fine, polyphonically-treated composition; he knows how to dispel the spirits he has raised, and bring the mind back to calm contemplation.

The various works which we have referred to above, have afforded many opportunities of pointing out the peculiarities of Brahms' work. Passing them once more in review, the prominent figure presented to us is that of a great and profoundly original creative genius. His essential feature is novelty of invention, both in motives and in melody, which is undoubtedly the ruling element in our modern music, and the distinctive mark of the man of genius.

Those who know only a little of Brahms' work will be surprised at his abundance of melody, and will often have cause to admire his clearness of form, his precision of rhythm and harmony, his versatility, and, lastly, the grave and noble dignity of his expression. It is not easy to explain precisely in what the beauty, the expression, in short the intrinsic value, of a truly original melody consists; it must be felt rather than put into words. The word melody, as we now understand it, originates from a dance-rhythm with words sung to it, and has gradually acquired its present meaning; hence we demand clearness of rhythm and precision as indispensable conditions of a good melody. But we require still further, in accordance with our present tone-system, a clear harmonic form. A fair variety of ascending and descending changes, moving in close or distant intervals, is not sufficient; the melody must move in a definite tonality, and every note of it must bear a fixed and perceptible relation to the principal key; or again—and this is the very basis of change—it should have a similar relation to the key-note of a nearly related key, to which one may modulate by a melodic transition.

It has also become a necessity with Lieder that their melody should be comprehensible and distinct, even without the aid of accompaniment. We can only understand this law, under our present musical system, as meaning that the harmonic basis which every note requires, and the harmonic relation of the individual notes, shall be such that the mind of the hearer can easily complete them. The natural complement of a note is found in the chord of the tonic, of which it can be the bass, the third, or the fifth, and those melodies are considered the most valuable and intelligible in which this harmonic completion takes place most simply and naturally. It is chiefly met with in popular melodies, and marks the inventive power of our best melodists. Brahms also goes upon this principle, and to express simple and natural sentiments makes use of this austere style of harmony. Consider for a moment the Old German Lied, in the songs Op. 43. The melody—unfortunately we cannot set it down here—moves easily to the words in the compass of a few notes, having the cadences of the periods in the nearest relative keys; but every note forms a constituent part of a tonic chord, whose bass indicates the key-note with infinite variety; and thus each note has a far greater weight than if it formed part of another chord, or of the preceding one, or again, than if it were merely an anticipated or passing note. Sometimes, and this tendency appears frequently (in the trio of the first string-quartet and elsewhere), Brahms constructs the melody within the notes of the scale, but every note is an essential part of a tonic chord. This affords many opportunities for variety of form according to the key in which the periods come to a close, whether the notes coming in succession belong to different chords or the same one; but we always find the emphasis of the melody based upon the tonic key-note of its constituent parts.

The chords of the seventh are weaker than the tonic chords, which naturally affects their melodic employment. When the notes are considered merely as anticipated or passing notes, more variety is obtained, but weakness and obscurity frequently result from this practice. The melodies of so many modern composers seem weak and expressionless because they too frequently make use of these commonplace progressions, even where strong and simple feelings are to be expressed, or because the closes of the periods are not clear and decisive, or repeat themselves monotonously in the same key, and because their rhythmic structure lacks precision and variety.

We have made these remarks, though we feel their incompleteness, to show in what respects we place Brahms in the first rank as a melodist possessed of true genius. We admire not only his wealth and variety of melodic invention, but also the artistic knowledge, the firm tact, with which his melodies are formed, elaborated, and adapted to the sense to be expressed. We learn from the study of Beethoven, and indeed it lies in the nature of things, that what appeals to us like a subtle, almost imperceptible fragrance, is, with a true artist, the result of the most assiduous consideration. Thus Brahms shows himself not only prolific and original in his inventive power, but he works with careful deliberation and unremitting severity, so much so, that at times his intellect seems forcibly to curb his imagination ; and yet, even in these cases, we are generally obliged to admit that it could not have been otherwise. Where the subject demands it, he is so austere and simple, that in some works (like the new motets) he seems almost to approach the old church-style; not that he desires to return to obsolete ideas, but that he occasionally combines some effects of the old-style with our modern system, which is absolute law to him. According to the text and character he wishes to express, he makes use of every means by which the modern system of harmony has made music more vigorous and more capable of interpreting complex feelings. He employs chromatic successions, and when the semitone is not used as an anticipated or passing note, modulates rapidly into the most distant keys; while anticipated notes are employed with decision and sure effect. We must add, what may indeed be easily gathered from all that has been said already, that while we always find in Brahms' inventive power something peculiar to himself, the ruling principle with him is, after all, a regard for pure musical form, and that never once, from the first moment of conscious power, has he exalted expression at the expense of beauty. In this respect, and especially in clearness, abundance, and beauty of melody, he closely follows Beethoven, while the naïve warm tone of his motives frequently recalls Schubert. Highly as Brahms honoured Schumann, and well as he knows how to employ the means of expression with which the latter enriched the art of music, he cannot, in our opinion, be classed as a follower of this master. It is to that fountain-head of all melody—national music, that he owes more than to any other example; it has yielded him all that is natural and original, and the truthfulness of his expression is ever being purified in this living stream. The decisive rhythm of his melodies, and his skill in alternating and combining a diversity of rhythmic forms, are parts of his originality. He has the art of adapting music to unusual and antique metres in a surprisingly clever way; of which we have already given several examples.

In a word, we may say that of all the inspired composers of the present day, Brahms approaches most nearly to Beethoven, recalling the traditions of this master in individuality, vigour, clearness of form, and in the ideal scope of his melodic inventions.

Any one who has attentively studied one of his great works, will observe that to his wealth of characteristic invention is added perfect musical science and an absolute mastery of technical resources. One great help towards a future development has fallen to Brahms' lot, in common with so many of our great composers. Thanks to a life spent among musical surroundings, he early acquired great execution as a pianist, and the habit of handling every variety of art-forms, possessions which he has since firmly secured by enlarged and assiduous study. In his earliest works we see him essaying the polyphonic style. The certainty and finish which he acquired in this style, enabling him to overcome its difficulties with playful ease, is noticeable not only in his great choral compositions, but in many of his instrumental works, of which we need only instance the last movement of the violoncello sonata, and the closing fugue of the Handel variations. It is not by mere accident that he has chosen this path; we know that among the masters who guided his youthful development J. Seb. Bach takes a prominent place, and it is the influence of this master which we may recognize in Brahms' polyphonically treated works. We need hardly add that in these also he makes full use of the resources of modern art; for nowadays no one would venture to write exactly like Bach.

Again, in his treatment of modulation, which we will also consider in this work, his method, though sensible to the influences of modern musical development, is thoroughly original. In this particular he is truly creative, a perfect master of the science of harmony, moving easily among the most remote keys, whose introduction always seems the natural result of the progression of the parts. We have already mentioned the pieces in which, in the simplest forms, by progressions of triads, he develops the harmony in a severe, almost harsh manner, especially when he gives every note of the diatonically constructed melody a harmonic basis. Where the expression requires it, he knows equally well how to use the chromatic and enharmonic modulation: and it is here that the peculiarities of Brahms' style will most forcibly impress the attentive listener. For instance, when the melody moves a semitone and touches a note not belonging to the scale of the key in use, he transposes the whole harmony to a higher key, and in this new tonality repeats the entire melody or a part of it; this is frequently done so simply and easily, that even with the most remote keys we are hardly struck by it. To understand our meaning clearly, the reader need only recall some of the Magelone romances, or the opening of the G Sextet. Other characteristics of his harmony are the easy, rapid change from major to minor; the use of the diminished triad in its first position (where the third is heard without inversion), and of the chords of the ninth and even the eleventh; also the employment of the key of the sub-dominant with the minor seventh at the close of a piece, and many other features which will not be lost upon the attentive observer. By means of harmonic transitions, he obtains that lustrous colouring, that warmth of expression, which strikes us in many of his songs, in his adagios and elsewhere.

From his cleverness in the management of form, we naturally pass to his skill in the construction of great works, in which respect, since the extravagance of the early period has been overcome, he has followed in the footsteps of Beethoven with ever increasing knowledge and certainty. The form remains as tradition has handed it down to us, and he makes no attempt to break through it, to the detriment of clearness. It is just in these great forms that his wealth of melody is best displayed. He skilfully invents contrasting themes, and in the movements of great dimensions often adds a third theme, while just as we are expecting the end new motives are revealed to us. In the "working out" sections Brahms does not follow Schumann, or the modern school, but only Beethoven, whom he rivals in the working of the themes. We have already noticed a few works of the first and second period, bearing traces of a conflict between imagination and reflection; yet on hearing these works frequently we become gradually enthralled by this strong artistic will. The ingenious manner in which he treated the coda has been already commented upon. The slow movements often take with him the form of variations; sometimes they consist of various parts, each having a distinct character, or sometimes a strongly-marked intermezzo breaks in upon the andante. Brahms shows great novelty and creative power in the structure of the Scherzo. The finale, especially in the greater works, is generally preceded by an introduction, a custom dating from Mozart's time. It occurs with striking effect in the first symphony.

We need not repeat how his dexterous management of form appears with even greater variety in the Songs.

All these characteristics, which might be enlarged upon in a detailed account of his works, flow from the individual nature of the artist, but can never exhaust its copious stream. This strong personality, without a flaw, soon reveals itself to those who study it without prejudice. But such impartiality is absolutely necessary in dealing with an artist who demands close investigation, and who repels those who think to understand him immediately and to appropriate at once all the secrets of his art.

In Brahms, we see before us an artist of the most serious nature, filled with the strongest sense of the dignity of his art. Since Beethoven, we hardly find any one so totally free from all that we may call trite and commonplace in music, as Brahms; and no artist possesses in so great a degree the virtue of self-restraint, or is so averse to all that fascinates by merely external or transient attractions. Those who expect in a work of art anything beyond art itself, must look elsewhere; they will never understand Brahms.

This artistic severity shows itself, not only in all that has been said about the treatment of technique, but also in the constant struggle after truth and a profoundly human expression; and though it is not easy to establish any rule here, we may call it the characteristic and tenour of his nature, that great and serious feelings have the strongest attraction for him, and that he is wonderfully successful in expressing them. Hence his predilection for religious subjects, and hence also the profound impressiveness of the Requiem and similar works. But everything he touches is ennobled by the truthfulness with which he grasps and renders the deepest feelings of the soul, by the rejection of all that is trivial and of merely subjective value, and by the pursuit of all that is simple and grand in humanity. Filled as he is with these deep feelings, he expresses them in the language of music, and thus obtains that naïveté and warmth of tone which so profoundly touches every student of Brahms' work. Indeed, in love-songs and compositions to similar words (the Magelone Lieder, for instance), he has never been equalled by any modern composer in warmth and genuine sentiment. This particular instance also shows how, even in this style, he willingly abandons himself to moments of serious reflection, and that it is not in his nature to be content with mere trifling. Elsewhere, however, where he rises above everyday life and lends his art to the highest and greatest purposes, he shows that austerity and harshness which demands from the hearer a zealous and earnest attention, but which brings its own reward.

We have now reached the point at which the individuality of the man and the artist become inseparably mingled. But in studying a living artist in the plenitude of his creative power, it is hazardous to look too far ahead—we must abstain from doing so; moreover it is no easy matter to delineate the individuality of a composer. All we can say is, that the individual development of an artist has much freer play now, than formerly, since his compositions result far less from external inspirations; and personal sentiments, derived directly from inward resources, now preponderate. Thus Brahms surprises us with every new work; no one can guess beforehand what he will produce next, and it is the desire of creation, the need of expressing the feelings of his inner life, that alone determines his compositions. Upon this basis rests the depth and genuine truthfulness of his works.

The time has not yet come to draw a parallel between Brahms and other modern composers — especially Schumann; it lies also beyond the province of this work. In such comparisons, we run this risk, that in extolling the characteristic qualities of one artist we deny to another some merit in which he is in reality not deficient; besides we are not yet in a position to form any such comparison with impartiality. Apart from the radical difference between the two men, which at once shows itself in their melodic invention, we must also remember the period which preceded Schumann, his efforts to reinstate in their proper dignity the poetic character of works of art, and to depose the shallowness and formality which then prevailed, to unite once again musical expression and profound sentiment. Hence the preponderance of imagination and the subjective tendency which characterized Schumann, especially in his early period, when, as he has said of himself, "the man and the musician strove to express themselves together." This tendency remained with him, accompanied however, at the climax of his development, by clearness and beauty of form which helped him to gain more intense and lasting effects. With Brahms this contrast never existed, except in some of his early attempts, and then only partially. His work, from the beginning, is naïve and simple, and displays no reformatory tendencies. What Schumann had felt the want of, Brahms found in abundance, perhaps even rather too strongly marked, in some followers of Schumann and Mendelssohn. For him there was but one thing needful, to obey his innate artistic impulse, and to give expression to his inspirations. This he did by means of those forms which, thanks to his early practice and assiduous study of the classical masters, he handled with such ease. If from the first he shows a strong objective tendency, if the requirements of the work of art itself are as law to him, we must attribute this as much to his natural disposition as to the altered circumstances of the art-world during the period which succeeded Beethoven's death, when Schumann and Mendelssohn first appeared.

Brahms' position in the musical world is not determined by a study of his compositions alone. As formerly we have seen him actively employed in promoting the performance of great works, especially Bach's, with devoted zeal, so we also find his name coupled with every undertaking which aimed at the preservation of the works of old and modern masters. He edited the piano compositions of Fr. Couperin for Chrysander's "Denkmäler der Tonkunst"; for the new edition of Mozart he undertook the revision of the Requiem; he was also concerned in the collected edition of Chopin's works. He edited three pieces, posthumous works of Schubert and a Scherzo and Presto Appassionato of Schumann's, arranged a Gavotte by Gluck for piano, also a Study of Chopin's, and finally a Rondo of Weber's for the "Studies for Pianoforte," published by Senff of Leipzig.

Were we to describe him as a pianist, we could prove that in that respect also he belongs to the first rank; to those true and genuine artists who, while having an absolute command of technique in all its branches, never make virtuosity the first object, but subordinate it to artistic ideas and the intellectual representation of the work.

In the present day we often hear the complaint that ideal aims and sentiments are dying out alike in life and in art. In consequence, we have of late frequently and justly remarked the necessity of taking strong measures to re-awaken a taste for art, and have endeavoured, by exaggerated realism and unnatural refinement of artistic means, to force a sentiment which can no longer be excited by the calm, peaceful influence of beauty. Unfortunately we see art, especially musical art, appealing to the basest and most superficial feelings, and, by exciting the senses, completely deadening the comprehension of the beautiful. At such a time we should be glad and thankful that we, in Germany, possess one artist of genius and inventive power, of profound education, full of enthusiasm for the true aim of art, and who, deriving his inspiration from Nature herself, despises everything petty and false, and earnestly seeks after the beautiful, the true, and the deeply human, endeavours to express them by his art, and thus helps, according to his means, to develop and maintain the intellectual welfare of our race. All who have the same aim in view should endeavour to understand him without prejudice, without attempts at comparison, or a desire to assign him his position in the history of music, which can only be done in future years. If we have frequently compared him to Beethoven, it was not with any idea of fixing his rank among the great masters; that is impossible in the present day. But we wished to express our convictions, which are shared by many others:

that Brahms, alone among our great contemporary composers, resembles Beethoven in style, in the forms of his compositions, and in workmanship, and that it is in Beethoven's footsteps that Brahms—most gifted of his successors—moves forward to the goal which every true artist has in view, and towards which every new creation brings him a step nearer.

BRAHMS' LATER COMPOSITIONS.

It will be seen that the foregoing publication appeared in Germany in 1880; this will explain why Brahms' latest compositions are not dealt with. Since that time upwards of twenty works have been published, which vary considerably in character and importance, but for the most part amply fulfil the magnificent promise of earlier years.

It is not intended to enter here upon a detailed criticism of these works; for any attempt at interpretation or exposition would need a far deeper musical culture and experience than the present writer possesses; but this little book would be incomplete without a short description of them, sufficient to point out their leading characteristics and tendencies.

First of all it is noticeable, in reviewing the works of the last seven years, that during this important period Brahms' style has undergone no very marked change, such as occasionally happens with great composers at their fullest maturity. Time has rather developed and confirmed his earlier characteristics than brought about any revolution in his modes of thought or expression. Though they are written in strict accordance with modern musical principles, these works display no startling innovations, no eccentricities of form or effect. Now, as formerly, Brahms remains distinctly conservative in his tendencies and methods.

He has further enriched and added to

every branch of art in which he has been previously successful; but as yet no dramatic work has been even hinted at, and it would be idle to speculate upon the possibility of this new departure. Still, with an artist endowed with such creative power, and withal so possessed of the virtue of reticence, it would be hard to say what the future may not have in store for us.

The works which immediately followed the Rhapsodies for piano (op. 79) were the two Orchestral Overtures first performed at a concert in Bremen, given in honour of Brahms when the University of that town conferred upon him the title of Doctor of Philosophy. The first of these compositions, " Academic Festival " (op. 80), was, as the title suggests, written expressly for this occasion. Based upon several popular student-songs, and winding up with the familiar " *Gaudeamus*," it was received with hearty enthusiasm in the Fatherland, where these tunes are known to every hearer; but the second, or "Tragic" Overture, seems to have won greater and more lasting favour in this country. This strong and serious work is couched in a gloomy tone; and its fine instrumentation and solid workmanship entitle it to a high place among Brahms' compositions. It speaks well for musical enterprise in England, that within a very few months of their first performance in Germany these works were heard, first at the Crystal Palace under the conductorship of Mr. Manns, and shortly afterwards at a Richter concert.

The Piano Concerto in B flat is a voluminous work in four movements, which has been aptly described as a "pianoforte symphony." Though presenting almost insuperable technical difficulties, it is brighter and more intelligible than its predecessor, and consequently more likely to win general appreciation.

We next come to the most important works of the last few years—the two Symphonies. Whether, judged by the standard of his other works, Brahms' symphonies entirely fulfil the requirements of this the highest form of instrumental music, is a question we cannot discuss here. The fact that so far only four have been offered to the world, has given colour to the suggestion that he rises with difficulty to the necessary elevation and grandeur of style. Some little time had elapsed since the appearance of the second symphony, and an expectant public awaited with interest the first performance of the third Symphony in F (op. 90). The work in question seems to combine some of the heroic and dignified qualities of the first Symphony in C with the more graceful and delicate character of the second in D. It opens with a majestic theme, which presently gives place to one, in direct contrast, of a graceful and pastoral nature, in A major. The intricate episodical details are worked out with consummate skill, but with such judicious restraint, that one of our best critics, Mr. C. A. Barry, has described this first movement as "a model of conciseness."

The slow movement, an Andante of enchanting melody, hardly sustains the epic character of the work, but appeals strongly to the ordinary hearer.

We are carried away by the Allegretto which follows—based on a theme in C minor in the so-called Lied-form. The piquantly-contrasting themes, and the easy grace and lucidity of this movement render it fascinating from beginning to end.

In the Finale, Brahms returns to a more elevated style. This time we feel that the composer is truly great and inspired, and this lofty mood finds its expression in a movement of exceptional grandeur, which, developed and completed with ever-increasing power and magnificence, rivets our attention from first to last. Taken as a whole the work leaves a profound impression, and seems to fulfil the great expectations awakened by its two predecessors.

The fourth Symphony in E minor (op. 98) has called forth a good deal of contradictory criticism. Like most of Brahms' works, it has, at first, its repellent, as well as its attractive side, and requires frequent hearing before it can be justly appreciated; even then it will only appeal to those who are content to find in music an intellectual exercise rather than a gratification of the senses.

The fourth Symphony was first performed at Meiningen, under the direction of Dr. von Bülow and Brahms himself, and was brought to a first hearing in England, while still in manuscript, at a Richter concert in May, 1886.

It opens with a melodious theme, quiet, and easily understood; this promise of simplicity, however, vanishes as the movement, carried out in Brahms' most scholarly style, gradually gains in interest, and also in complexity and variety of treatment. Yet in spite of numerous contrasting subjects and intricate development there is no diffuseness, no halting by the way; the main idea is kept clearly before us throughout this difficult and stirring movement, in the energetic purpose and virile force of which, we may recognize the stamp of Brahms' distinct individuality.

The Andante does not call for special attention. It is, perhaps, one of the most beautiful movements Brahms ever wrote, and speaks for itself, alike to the learned and unlearned, by its melodic charm, its warmth of tone and genuine inspiration.

Evading the strictly classical lines, the composer gives in place of a scherzo a third movement in the Rondo form (*allegro giocoso*) full of animation and spirit. With the sprightly audacity of the opening theme is contrasted one of a more sober character.

The Finale takes quite a novel form, being a development of the form known as that of the Passacaglia, a form which, unlike those of most of its fellows, the movements of the Suite, had never been previously introduced into the symphonic structure. A theme of eight bars long is treated persistently throughout the movements, in a manner resembling the characteristic method of procedure with variations, and displaying ever-increasing contrapuntal skill and intricacy of detail.

Reviewing this work in its entirety,

it seems, with its cleverly constructed first and last movements, in which scientific knowledge, though it predominates over imagination, never degenerates to mere dry-as-dust erudition, and its human and heart-felt middle movements, whose beauties are accessible to all, to include, more completely than any of the later compositions, those rare combinations of emotion and intellect, of modern feeling and old-fashioned skill, which are the distinguishing features of Brahms' style.

By far the greater number of Brahms' later works consist of vocal pieces for one or more voices; indeed, since 1880 no less than eight books of songs have appeared, exclusive of numerous quartets and romances for mixed chorus. His predilection for song-writing seems to grow stronger year by year, and perhaps nowhere more than in his songs does his powerful personality make itself felt.

The choice of words for his later, as for his earlier, songs shows the same thoughtful tact, and is of itself an index to the character of the man. Always avoiding the commonplace, he sometimes passes by what seems most beautiful and suitable for musical interpretation, and fixing on an apparently unpromising poem, addresses himself with characteristic energy to the task of investing it with deep musical purpose and expression. Some of his finest songs have words valuable in sense, but unattractive in sound.

Of the three collections—Op. 84-86—those in the first book, Five Songs and Romances with PF. accompaniment, are treated in the style of little dramatic scenes between two people, as mother and daughter, maiden and lover, but may be sung indifferently by one or two voices. The first three are settings of verses by Hans Schmidt, one of which

—'Sommerabend'—recalls in character an earlier favourite "*O versenk.*" The two last—"Lower Rhenish Volkslieder"—are happy examples of Brahms' naïve and sympathetic treatment of more popular subjects. The Six Songs (op. 85), with words by Heine, Siegfried Kapper, Geibel and Lemcke, are all highly interesting. Full of poetic beauty are the settings of Heine's '*Sommerabend*' (Summer Eve) and *Mondenschein* (Moonbeams); while the '*Servian Maiden's Song*,' with its unusual time-signature—$\frac{5}{4}$, afterwards $\frac{6}{4}$—is strikingly original. In the third book we find the greatest variety of character and sentiment, ranging from the playful humour of Gottfried Keller's "*Du milchjunger Knabe*" (Thou forward young fledgling), to the profound expression of sadness and weariness in von Schenkendorff's '*Todessehnen*' (Shadows of Death).

Two Songs for Alto with viola obbligato (op. 91) are perfect examples of Brahms' genius as a song-writer, and seem to call for special attention. "No one," says Dr. E. Hanslick in a very clever and sympathetic criticism of these songs, "will assume that Brahms has inserted the viola obbligato without purpose, or merely as a sort of musical sugar-plum. He uses the viola here as an important, even indispensable, means of expression. In Rückert's poem 'Longing at Rest,' it seems to prepare the way in a long melodious symphony, characteristic of the 'golden light of evening,' for the monologue which follows. Later on it suggests, in soft, lulling sextolets, the birds and breezes which 'whisper the world to sleep.' It plays the same double part of musical adornment and poetical interpretation in the still more remarkable 'Cradle Song of the Virgin.' Between the voice-part and the piano accompaniment glides like a silver thread the simple and touching melody of a very old song, '*Joseph lieber Joseph mien, hilf mir wiegen mein Kindlein fein.*' These are songs which do not reveal the full power of their charm at a first hearing, as do those of Schubert but their exquisite spirit possesses us longer and more forcibly, and seems ever to reveal new underlying beauties."

Five Songs (op. 94) are written in a thoughtful and affecting mood. Almost painfully expressive of suffering is the setting of Geibel's "*Mein Herz ist schwer*" (My heart is sad); and the little song by F. Halm, "No Home, no Country," is also very pathetic. The graceful 'Sapphic Ode' will probably gain more general approbation.

Seven Songs (op. 95) are simpler as regards sentiment and musical technique. We might instance the one entitled,

"*Mein Schatz ist ein Jäger,*" which overflows with joyous life; and again, by way of contrast, the impassioned song which closes the book, "*Schön war's, das ich dir weihte Das goldne Geschmeide.*"

Of the Four Songs (op. 96), three are settings of short poems by Heine. These are exquisite, lyrical gems, delicately handled, concise in construction and truly inspired.

In the Six Songs (op. 97)—very recently published—Brahms treats a variety of subjects, but each song bears the stamp of his individuality. The fresh and spirited Lower Rhenish Volkslied, "There among the Willows," and the touching Swabian song, "Parting," afford two characteristic examples of Brahms' sympathy with popular sentiment, both in its playful and in its more serious aspects. The remarkable song " O Lady Judith," is pervaded with a spirit of mediæval romance.

The book of Quartets (op. 92) contains, among other things, a very clever setting of Goethe's little poem, "*Warum.*" Six Songs and Romances for four-part chorus (op. 93) open with an old Rhenish Volkslied—" The Humpbacked Fiddler." This characteristic sketch is full of genuine humour. A young, humpbacked fiddler, journeying homewards, meets some lovely ladies by the way, who beg him to play them his liveliest dance-tune. He complies with their request, and when the dance is over they show their gratitude by spiriting away his hump. A more serious composition is No. 2, a graceful servian song by Siegfried Kapper, entitled "The Maiden."

Another work for six-part mixed chorus and PF. accompaniment is Eichendorff's "*Tafellied*" (Dank der Damen, op. 93 b). The light and complimentary verses are tossed backwards and forwards—if we may use the expression—between the men's and women's voices, in a kind of musical battledore and shuttlecock which is capable of charming effect, if well and brightly rendered.

The relentlessness of Fate is the subject which has inspired Brahms' two latest choral works: a setting of Schiller's poem '*Nänie*,' and the *Gesang der Parzen* (Song of the Fates), from Goethe's " Iphigenia." And when we consider that one of the most perfect compositions of his earlier days, the " Song of Destiny," owes its origin to the same subject, it seems as though it offered some very strong attraction to his serious and reflective nature. "*Nänie*," a choral ode, was first given in England in March, 1883, but did not meet with a very cordial reception. It probably suffered from a natural, but somewhat unfair, comparison with Goetz's more attractive setting of the same poem.

Brahms has often shown his liking for classical subjects, and his power of reproducing their calm spirit with conscientious truthfulness and intelligence. In this clever, but inanimate, composition, he seems to have exaggerated this tendency till it becomes a fault. There is, at times, in the 'Nänie,' an obvious want of sympathy between the words and the music; and the reason for this is not far to seek. Throughout Schiller's poem runs a vein of subjective sentiment, a suggestion of regretful and human pity—" The gods and the goddesses all mourn that the beautiful fades,"—and it is the reproduction of this milder feeling that we miss in the stern and scholarly formality of the music to the " Nänie."

But if in the "Nänie" Brahms has pushed this frigid classicism beyond the requirements of the text, the same fault cannot be found with the Parzenlied; and for a different reason. Goethe was so entirely penetrated by the antique spirit, that scarcely a trace of modern feeling is observable in his handling of classical subjects. Of this same "Iphigenia" it has been well said that it was beautiful as marble, and as cold. The chilly musical atmosphere in which Schiller's poem is unsuitably enveloped, is not out of place when it environs the severe and purely classical text of the author of the "Achilleid." The music, pervaded by a spirit of gloomy foreboding and hopeless doubt, is profoundly impressive. But, with all its merits, the Parzenlied can never become popular; partly because of the difficulties which the chorus presents, but chiefly because it is, as may well be imagined, utterly deficient in what are considered attractive qualities. Even those robust minds who can appreciate Brahms in his moods of most uncompromising severity, will feel repelled on first hearing this work; which, of all his compositions, seems to proceed most directly from the intellect rather than the imagination.

There have been several recent additions to his chamber-music. First in order of publication come the Trio in C, for PF., violin, and cello (op. 87), a work of great vigour, somewhat wanting in the more attractive qualities ; and the string Quintet in F (op. 88.) The latter was written during a summer sojourn at Ischl, in 1882, and was first heard in England at one of Mr. Henry Holmes' concerts. Besides a considerable display of contrapuntal skill, there is plenty of animation and colour about the work, so that on the whole it excites both pleasure and interest. The joyous and tuneful character of the first movement is especially winning, while the last fugal movement is worked out in a truly masterly manner.

R. N.

During the musical season of 1887, no

less than three new works of this class have been heard in London:—a sonata in F for pianoforte and violoncello (op. 99); another in A for pianoforte and violin (op. 100); and a trio in C minor for pianoforte and strings (op. 101). These productions must be regarded as a new and most important addition to the evidence of their author's greatness. A very distinct advance has been made in the direction of clearness and intelligibility, while no falling off in originality or power has to be recorded. For absolute beauty, too, these works will hold their own against any other group of the master's compositions. Amongst them the palm must, in this respect, be awarded to the violin sonata, which cannot fail to give very great pleasure even at first hearing.

The violoncello sonata is like the proverbial month of March in the manner of its ingress and egress. Its first movement is mysterious and gloomy, while the last carries us away with its irrepressible good-humour and merriment. Between these two extremes comes a very beautiful slow movement, in which a pizzicato figure for the stringed instrument plays a prominent part, and a passionate scherzo with a very genial trio. The collocation of keys is an exceedingly curious feature of this sonata, and all the more so since Brahms' conservatism in such matters is well known. That a work in F major should have its slow movement in F sharp major is, we believe, without parallel in music, but it cannot be said to have anything but a good effect. A kind of prophecy of the key of the adagio is to be found at the beginning of the working-out section of the first movement, when the extraneous key of F sharp minor is reached by an extremely ingenious device.

The violin sonata shows us the composer in his most genial mood. It would almost seem that the combination of violin and pianoforte suggested to him a certain idyllic tenderness and gentle pathos such as are not frequent elsewhere in his works. These are at least the qualities which both violin sonatas have in common, and which distinguish them from all the rest of his chamber-music. As in the case of the sonata in G, the opening of the new work strikes us by its simplicity and artlessness. The only structural novelty admitted into the first part is the device of echoing the last bar of each strain, so that the theme falls into sections of five bars instead of four. It is some time before the characteristic combination of triple with duple rhythms begins, but when it does, with the second subject of the movement, it carries everything before it, generating all kinds of beautiful passages (note the exquisite episode in C sharp minor, than which even Brahms has written no lovelier or more haunting melody). The middle section of the sonata contains a slow movement and a scherzo, which continually interrupt one another, so that the pathetic andante, if it had not preceded the entry of the scherzo, might have been mistaken for its trio. The result of this experiment is exceedingly happy, and the alternation of wild gaiety with passionate earnestness is managed with infinite skill. The final movement presents us with a contrast between a placid strain of melody of a character easily appreciated, and a gloomy stream, dark with vague and mysterious harmonies; the use of a similar contrast will be remembered in the "Tragic" overture.

The new trio exhibits the other side of the composer's character. Like its predecessor the trio in C (op. 87), it is full of vigour and masculine energy. But its appeal to the intellect of the hearer is far more direct, and its form is far more easily intelligible, than is the case with that work. Its first movement has some characteristics in common with the corresponding part of the F minor quintet, but the beautiful breadth shown in the treatment of the second subject is not found in the earlier work. The scherzo, played *con sordini* by the strings, is full of interest, in spite of its short extent. An important episode, consisting of massive chords, arranged in a curiously unexpected rhythm, serves as a foreboding of the slow movement, in which the composer's fondness for rhythmic peculiarities is indulged to the full. A strong evidence of his power and freedom is found in the ease with which he uses what is practically seven-crochet time (for the sake of convenience it is printed as a bar of 3-4, followed by two of 2-4), and makes it sound as if it were the most natural thing in the world. An impulsive and extraordinarily original finale brings the whole to a worthy conclusion.—EDITOR.

Early this year (1887), the Emperor William, in acknowledgment of Herr Brahms' exceptional talents, appointed him Knight of the Order "pour le mérite" for Arts and Sciences; and wherever he goes in Germany, the enthusiastic receptions accorded to him show that this esteem is shared by the majority of his countrymen.

In conclusion it remains to be said that the translation of this work was undertaken with the desire of helping those who, honestly seeking to arrive at a clearer understanding of Brahms' music, have found him at times unapproachable and obscure. Should it do this, and help to pave the way for a more intelligent appreciation of such noble works of art, it will have more than fulfilled the hopes of the translator.

LIST OF BRAHMS' PUBLISHED WORKS TO MAY, 1887.

OPUS.
1. Sonata for PF. in C.
2. Sonata for PF. in F sharp minor.
3. Six Songs.
4. Scherzo for PF. in E flat minor.
5. Sonata for PF. in F minor.
6. Six Songs for Soprano or Tenor.
7. Six Songs.
8. Trio in B, PF., Violin and Violoncello.
9. Variations for PF. on a Theme by Schumann.
10. Four Ballades for PF.
11. Serenade for Full Orchestra in D.
12. Ave Maria for Female Voices, Orchestra and Organ.
13. Funeral Hymn for Chorus and Wind.
14. Eight Songs and Romances.
15. Concerto in D for PF. and Orchestra.
16. Serenade for Small Orchestra in A.
17. Four Songs for Female Chorus, Two Horns, and Harp.
18. Sextet in B flat for Strings.
19. Five Poems for Voice and PF.
20. Three Duets for Soprano and Alto with PF.

OPUS.
21. Variations for PF. :
    (1) On an Original Theme.
    (2) On a Hungarian Melody.
22. Seven "Marienlieder" for Four-part Chorus, in Two Books.
23. Variations for PF., four hands, on a Theme by Schumann.
24. Variations and Fugue for PF. on a Theme by Handel.
25. Quartet in G minor for PF. and Strings.
26. Quartet in A for ditto.
27. Psalm XIII. for Women's Voices, with Organ or PF.
28. Four Duets for Alto and Baritone with PF.
29. Two Motets for Five Voices, *a capella*.
30. Sacred Song by Paul Flemming, for Four-part Chorus and Organ.
31. Three Quartets for S. A. T. B.
32. Nine Songs by A. von Platen and G. F. Daumer. For Voice and PF. in Two Books.
33. Fifteen Romances from Tieck's "Magelone," for Voice and PF. in Five Books.
34. Quintet for PF. and Strings in F minor.
34* Sonata for PF. for four hands from the above.
35. Twenty-eight Variations (Studien) for PF. on a Theme by Paganini.

OPUS.
36. Sextet in G for Strings.
37. Three Sacred Choruses for Female Voices.
38. Sonata in E minor for PF. and Violoncello.
39. Sixteen Waltzes for PF.; four hands.
40. Trio in E flat for PF., Violin and Horn (or Violoncello).
41. Five Part Songs for Four Men's Voices.
42. Three Songs for six-part Chorus, *a capella.*
43. Four Songs for One Voice and PF.
44. Twelve Songs and Romances for Female Chorus, *a capella.*
45. German Requiem, for Soli, Chorus, and Orchestra.
46. Four Songs with PF. accompaniment.
47. Four ditto.
48. Seven ditto.
49. Five ditto.
50. Rinaldo; Cantata by Goethe, for Tenor Solo, Male Chorus and Orchestra.
51. Two Quartets for Strings, in C minor and A minor.
52. Liebeslieder-Walzer for PF. duet and four voices.
53. Rhapsodie; fragment from Goethe's "Harzreise" for Alto Solo, Male Chorus and Orchestra.

OPUS.

54. Schicksalslied (Song of Destiny), by F. Hölderlin, for Chorus and Orchestra.
55. Triumphlied (Rev. chap. xix.) for Eight-part Chorus and Orchestra.
56. Variations on a Theme by Haydn for Orchestra.
56*Variations on a Theme by Haydn for Two Pianos.
57. Eight Songs by Daumer.
58. Eight Songs.
59. Eight ditto.
60. Quartet (No. 3) in C minor for PF. and Strings.
61. Four Duets for Soprano and Alto.
62. Seven Songs for Four-part Chorus.
63. Nine Lieder und Gesänge.
64. Three Quartets for Four Solo Voices and PF.
65. Neue Liebeslieder-Walzer.
66. Five Duets.
67. String Quartet in B flat.
68. Symphony No. 1, in C. minor.
69. Nine Songs.
70. Four Songs.
71. Five Songs.
72. Five Songs.
73. Symphony No. 2, in D.

OPUS.

74. Two Motets.
75. Ballads and Romances for Two Voices.
76. Eight Pieces (Capriccios and Intermezzi) for PF.
77. Concerto for Violin.
78. Sonata for PF. and Violin in G.
79. Two Rhapsodies for PF.
80.
81. Two Overtures for Orchestra (No. 1, "Academic Festival"; No. 2, "Tragic" in D minor).
82. Nänie; from a Poem of Schiller's, for Chorus and Orchestra.
83. Concerto for PF. No. 2 in B flat.
84. Lieder.
85. Ditto.
86. Ditto.
87. Trio for PF., Violin and Violoncello in C.
88. Quintet for Strings in F.
89. Gesang der Parzen; from Goethe's "Iphigenia," for Six-part Chorus and Orchestra.
90. Symphony No. 3 in F.
91. Two Songs for Contralto, with Viola Obbligato.
92. Four Quartets for Solo Voices and PF.
93. Six Songs and Romances for Four-part Chorus.
93*Eichendorff's "Tafellied" for Six-part Chorus.
94. Five Songs.

OPUS.
95. Seven Songs.
96. Four Songs.
97. Six Songs.
98. Symphony No. 4 in E minor.
99. Sonata in F for PF. and Violoncello.
100. Sonata in A for PF. and Violin.
101. Trio in C minor for PF., Violin and Violoncello.

Without Opus Number :—
Hungarian Dances for PF., duet.
The same for Orchestra.
Gluck's Gavotte in A, arranged for PF. Solo.
Studies for PF. Solo :
    (1) Etude after Chopin ;
    (2) Rondo after Weber.
Fifteen Volkskinderliedchen.
Mondnacht. Song.
Choralvorspiel for Organ.
Fugue for Organ.

For EU product safety concerns, contact us at Calle de José Abascal, 56–1°, 28003 Madrid, Spain or eugpsr@cambridge.org.

www.ingramcontent.com/pod-product-compliance
Ingram Content Group UK Ltd.
Pitfield, Milton Keynes, MK11 3LW, UK
UKHW041953230426
12048UKWH00008B/309